C60025235 Z

D1102933

THE 80/20 DIET

THE 80/20 DIET

12 weeks to a better body
TERESA CUTTER

Photography by Paul Cutter

MURDOCH BOOKS

Acknowledgements

Many thanks to Kay Scarlett for her encouragement and support with this book. Also thanks to Janine Flew and Margaret Malone for editing the tonnes of information I blurted out on paper, and to Vivien Valk for her art direction.

Thanks also to my wonderful husband Paul Cutter, who has been my driving force and a tremendous support for the last 16 years of our life together. You're a beautiful, talented individual and maker of dreams. You complete my life and our books with your unconditional love and eye for beauty. My little angel … your photos in this book look amazing!

Thanks to Doctor Anish Singh from Metabolic Medicine, whom I've had the pleasure of knowing and learning from for the last 15 years. Your passion for health, fitness and prevention of disease is paramount. Thank you for all the support you have given me.

Thanks also to Doctor Albina Della Bruna, a wonderful friend and healer. Your passion for helping others is inspirational. Thank you for all your wonderful support and wisdom.

Last but not least, thank you to Jamie Short and Darren Shaw from Ignite Health, for being so supportive to Paul and myself, as well as being taste testers for a lot of the recipes in this book.

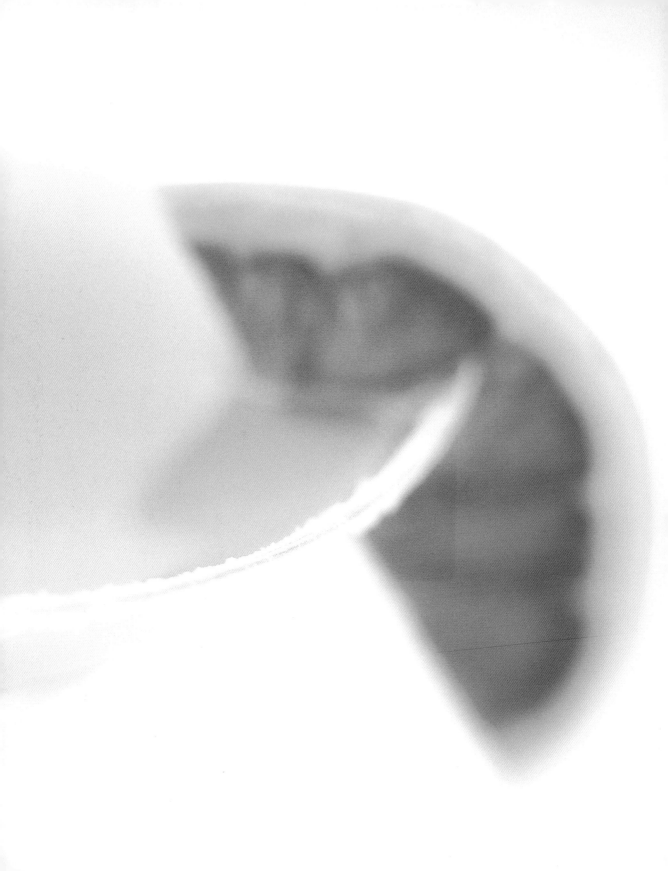

Contents

Introduction

The inspiration behind this book

In 2004, I finished filming a segment called 'Get On Track Australia' for *A Current Affair* on Australia's Channel 9. I was asked to design a healthy eating plan to help three brave women lose their unwanted weight. They allowed the cameras to film their progress and the results to be televized to the whole country.

The women did really well, losing between 5 and 7 kg (11 and 15 lb) each in only six weeks of sticking to the diet and getting some low-impact exercise. The transformations were amazing and the women were ecstatic. All three women are now well on their way to a healthier, happier life and have gained the knowledge that will help keep them on track. In addition, another 25,205 Australians took part in the campaign, losing an amazing nationwide total of 6002 kg (13,228 lb).

This success of the program was the inspiration behind this book. I felt that people needed to know that it takes only a few changes to their lifestyle and eating habits to see real improvements in health and wellbeing — that, and a little bit of dedication! I hope the 80/20 diet provides you with all the motivation you need to get on track for a healthy and fit new you that can be maintained for the rest of your life.

My background

When people ask me how I got into all of this, what influenced my love of cooking and what started me on my own health regime, I sometimes feel a little silly telling them how young I was when it all began. I started helping out in my aunt's kitchen when I was about four years old and embarked on my health crusade when I was nine years old!

My great-aunt was a good cook and baker; she would mix cakes by hand with a wooden spoon and churn out *babka* and *sernik* on a weekly basis for our Polish family and friends. I would watch her and help out in the kitchen; she would get me to sift the flour, prepare all the ingredients and shape *piroshki* with my tiny fingers. This was the beginning of my love of cooking.

Food was a big deal in our household; there were always extra-large portions and second helpings, coated with lots of butter. At the age of nine, I realized I was overweight. A group of high-school students were doing a survey and they recorded the weight and height of our class. I was shocked to discover that I was the heaviest in the class; 10–15 kg (22–33 lb) more than most of my classmates. I remember that day as if it were yesterday. It changed my life forever and was the inspiration for what I do today.

The very next day I asked my mother to buy more fruit and vegetables for me to eat and to buy a healthier breakfast cereal with fibre and less sugar. I started refusing deep-fried foods, which forced Mum into practising healthier cooking methods with our meals. Instead of catching the school bus, I began to walk to school. From then on, I'd walk straight past the shops after school instead of popping in and buying bagfuls of mixed lollies or ice creams, as I used to do every day.

I'd never really participated in much sport, but I enrolled myself in the school netball and basketball teams and tried out all sorts of fun school sports when we had carnivals. My aunt and uncle bought me my first bicycle and encouraged me to go riding with them regularly. They were in their late fifties at the time, had never owned a car and used to ride their bikes or walk everywhere. I think their example inspired my later love of bicycle racing.

I remember watching shows such as the *Richard Simmons Show* in school holidays and joining in with the exercises. I also experimented with the healthy recipes they made on these shows. I made my first egg-white omelette and showed Mum that if you drain the juices from a roast chicken and put them in the refrigerator, you'll be able to skim off all the excess saturated fat and make a delicious gravy just by thickening the juices with a little cornflour (cornstarch). Without realizing it, I had lost all the excess fat within a year. I felt great! I felt fit and healthy for the first time. I could move around freely and not puff and pant. I was eating healthily and exercising regularly, and, as a result, was happy and full of energy.

The 80/20 philosophy

Today I am a qualified chef and personal trainer, and have combined my knowledge of nutrition, diet and exercise to specialize in developing healthy recipes and training clients for fat loss, toning and body shaping. My recipes are simple, nutritious dishes that are low in fat and high in flavour, and they have been designed for people who love food, who love to eat and who have made a conscious decision to maximize their health and wellbeing. My program is a well-balanced, easy-to-follow eating and exercise regime that you can manage for the rest of your life. It's about knowing your body, indulging those cravings once in a while, including moderate daily exercise and enjoying life.

After working in food and fitness for so many years I have seen what works and what doesn't, and what's just a temporary fix. Most of us gain weight for three reasons. We eat way too much, we eat the wrong foods, and we don't move enough. Next time you go grocery shopping, take a good look inside the other trolleys around you. Then take a good look at the people pushing them. You decide!

In an ideal world, it would be great if we could all eat healthily 100 per cent of the time. But if I can get people to eat healthily 80 per cent of the time, then I've made a difference and we can help reverse the current trend towards obesity. That's the simple philosophy of the 80/20 diet — eat well 80 per cent of the time, and 20 per cent of the time you can enjoy a little indulgence. So six days a week, try eating foods that are good for the body. Think about what you put into your body. For fat loss, the recipes are specifically designed to provide the right carbohydrates at the right time of day. Those of us who eat too many carbohydrates will burn those in preference to fat; consequently, fat-burning is not activated and weight loss becomes difficult. If the right carbohydrates are eaten at the right time of day and you supply your body with enough healthy food, then your body will allow fat to be burnt. Eat most of your good carbs combined with a little protein for breakfast and lunch, when you are most active. Dinner should be a mix of water-based, high-fibre, lower-carbohydrate vegetables and protein.

Make one day a week your 20 per cent. That's the day you can indulge your favourite cravings and eat what you like — *in moderation*. It's not a licence to pig out; it's about having one or two chocolate biscuits, or four little squares of dark chocolate, on a Saturday night — not the whole packet or block. Eat enough to satisfy your sweet tooth, not enough to make you gain more body fat or make you feel sick. I just want to make it very clear that it's 20 per cent once a week, not 20 per cent every day. This will allow you to nourish your body with good foods and give you the best opportunity to lose weight and burn body fat.

This diet and exercise plan is based on positive action and disease prevention, making us responsible for our own health and wellbeing. It doesn't matter if you have a lot of fat to lose or just need to take a little off your tummy, legs and arms; it is suitable for everybody. After 12 weeks of following the 80/20 diet and getting regular exercise, you'll be leaner, your body will be more toned and you'll feel fantastic and energized. You'll also have discovered a program that is so easy to follow, you will be able to continue this lifestyle for the rest of your life.

Be patient, be consistent and listen to your body

These are the three essentials to being able to lose body fat and maintain a healthy lifestyle. Most people expect to see instant results — perhaps this is because of all the fad diets around promising reductions of 10 kg (22 lb) in just one week. But such diets fail because people can't sustain the ultra-low-calorie strict eating demands for long periods. They have no energy, and feel grumpy and lousy. Quick-fix low-calorie diets cause a rapid loss not only of fat but also of essential muscle tissue. Everyone is out for the instant fix! But the reality is that although quick-fix diets may cause a speedy weight loss, this usually leads to speedy weight gain soon after.

Losing fat takes time, effort and commitment. You should enjoy the good food you're putting into your body and every once in a while indulge your cravings, enjoy them in moderation without feeling guilty, and move on. The 80/20 diet is all about helping you achieve your weight loss goals sensibly and establishing a healthy lifestyle that can be maintained for the rest of your life.

Take care of your body and yourself. Live the life you've imagined.

What is the 80/20 diet?

The 80/20 diet is all about eating a balanced healthy diet necessary for losing body fat sensibly, and establishing an exercise and lifestyle program that can be maintained for life. Eat well 80 per cent of the time, and 20 per cent of the time you can enjoy a little indulgence. Weight gain and weight loss are both cumulative over time, as it's what you do in the long term that counts most of all. The 80/20 diet will allow you to maintain a healthy eating and exercise plan for the rest of your life.

The 80/20 diet is an uncomplicated program designed for the busy person who hasn't got the time to fuss over complicated foods and recipes. The healthy recipes are crafted for people who love food, love to eat and who have made a conscious decision to maximize their health and wellbeing. The diet introduces balance into everyday life, and at the same time allows the odd indulgence. Now I'm not saying it's going to be easy. It will take a certain amount of discipline and effort on your behalf. This book is designed to take you out of your comfort zone and provide you with the tools to healthier eating and a healthier lifestyle. Your body will thank you for it!

I've trained a lot of people who've worked hard all their lives building up their businesses and family lifestyle. By the time they reach their mid thirties to forties, they're overweight, stressed-out workaholics and their health starts to suffer. If this is the case with you, it's important to put time aside for yours truly.

Look after yourself and your body will look after you.

Being healthy and fit is something we all have to work at every day for the rest of our lives, and by looking after ourselves first we are then able to look after others properly.

The 80/20 diet is what I live by every day — now it's time for you to put yourself first and take up the challenge!

Relaxation and good-quality sleep are essential for the body and mind to revive and recharge. They provide a healing balance of mind, body and soul.

THE IMPORTANCE OF A MEDICAL CHECKUP

Before changing your diet and starting any fitness regime, I strongly recommend you get checked out by your medical practitioner. Make sure this is a detailed full-body check, including extensive blood analysis; that way you'll be able to rectify any deficiencies in vitamins such as iron, folate or B12, or hormone imbalances such as high insulin levels, that can effect not only fat loss but also your energy levels and feeling of wellbeing. I personally have a full-body check every year to keep my body on track.

The three keys to the 80/20 diet

There are three key parts to the 80/20 diet. The first part is the food. You can choose recipes from each of the recipe chapters and follow your own meal plan, or if you like a more structured program, I've also included a 12-week menu plan to make life a bit easier. You decide which one suits you. You definitely are what you eat, and eating good nutritious food will keep your body lean, beautiful and healthy.

Secondly, exercise is crucial to the 80/20 diet. All you need is 60 minutes a day, five or six days a week. Moderate exercise will increase your metabolism and strengthen your body and immune system, making you more resistant to disease and illness. Lastly, you need adequate rest and relaxation.

Food

Eating fresh, nutritious food is the cornerstone of good health. The recipes in the 80/20 diet are low in saturated fats, salt and refined sugar, and high in nutrients. They contain an abundance of fresh vegetables and fruit, lean protein, wholegrains, nuts, seeds, and plenty of water to maintain adequate hydration at all times.

The recipes are simple and easy to prepare, so the food retains most of its nutrients. The cooking is done with little or no oil, instead using stock or water to retain the moisture and flavour in the food. The recipes are designed to appeal to everybody and many are suitable even for those with allergies and food intolerances. There are also some yummy vegetarian recipes, so there are no excuses — there is something here for everyone. It's all about enjoying the food you love, nourishing your body and losing fat.

The basis of this diet is the 80/20 concept. About 80 per cent of the time, you need to stick to good eating habits, eating lots of vegetables, lean protein, fresh fruit, wholegrains, nuts and seeds. Remember, no starches such as pasta, rice, noodles, potato or bread at night. If you're going to eat these starches, introduce them for breakfast and lunch where they can be burned off during the day. I'm not saying these foods are bad, because they're not; but where most people go wrong is that they eat way too much of them — much more than the portion size of half a cup. So remember, if you want to indulge in foods such as pasta, control your portions, eat it for lunch and eat it with a nice, low-fat tomato-based sauce. No carbonara, Alfredo or other creamy sauces.

About 20 per cent of the time — or roughly one day a week — you can indulge your favourite cravings. So, for example, for six days a week, you'll eat well, do your exercise training and stick to a regular, healthy routine. Then one day a week you can basically choose to do and eat whatever you want. But it's important to remember portion control — the 20 per cent is not a licence to binge, but a chance to eat sensibly the foods you like. Enjoy that chocolate cake or crème brûlée if you want — but eat it in moderation and then move on. This way you won't feel like you're missing out on anything, which will make it possible for you to sustain good eating habits for the rest of your life. In fact, you may eventually find that after a while you won't crave fatty, sugary foods, but will want to exercise and eat healthily most of the time. If you have to go out midweek for dinners and functions, you will need willpower, but just order sensibly and stick to leafy salads or steamed vegetables and lean protein such as seafood, with sauces and dressings on the side.

If you're really serious about losing weight, give alcohol the flick and keep it as one of your 20 per cent, once-a-week foods. It's second only to fat in the amount of kilojoules (calories) that it contains; also, it has no nutritive value, it affects the absorption of vitamins, minerals and essential fatty acids, increases digestive problems, causes liver damage and weakens the immune system. Alcohol also weakens our willpower, so you're more likely to eat fatty foods and will find it hard to get up early the next day and participate in your morning exercise.

Remember that you need to give yourself plenty of time. Fat loss is not a quick process — it requires effort and commitment over the long term.

Exercise

The 80/20 diet encourages regular exercise — ideally, at least five days a week. You should enjoy your exercise — it's important to make it fun, especially if it's going to become part of your everyday lifestyle.

It's important to do a combination of cardio, resistance training and flexibility training to ensure overall fitness and body shaping. The cardio will get you fit and help you lose body fat. The resistance training will help you increase your metabolic rate by encouraging the growth of lean muscle mass, and it's one of the best ways to encourage your body to use more fat as fuel. Studies show that even a loss of 25 g (1 oz) of muscle tissue can lower your metabolic rate and reduce your ability to burn body fat efficiently.

Resistance training will also help shape and sculpt your body. So, if you want toned arms and shoulders, toned legs, a flat tummy and a perky, firm bottom, you need to do resistance training.

Flexibility training (stretching) will help decrease muscle soreness and increase mobility, which will reduce the incidence of injury. Stretching also encourages the release of toxins in the muscles and increases the supply of blood and nutrients to that area. Basically, being flexible will help you perform better and enjoy life a lot more.

At the back of this book I provide a number of exercise routines you can do at home or in the gym, but the key is to work out a program that is right for you. Whatever you do, try to vary your routine and make it interesting; that way you won't get bored. Challenge yourself and set goals, and work hard. I want you to aim for 60 minutes a day, even if you have to split them up into two sessions: one morning session and another after work.

Now I'm not talking about running marathons here. Listen to your body and note how you feel. Try to have 3–4 good sessions a week broken up with 2–3 moderate to light sessions. If you've pushed it a bit hard one day and your body is tired, have a rest day, go for a light walk or have a massage. Remember it's what you do over the long term that counts, as exercise and good nutrition have a cumulative effect on the body. You may experience a little muscle soreness in the first few weeks on the exercise program, but that will soon ease off as your body gets used to the routine.

Just remember, if you want to change the shape of your body, you're going to have to put in the hard effort.

Rest and relaxation

Rest, relaxation and good-quality sleep are essential for the body and mind to revive, repair and recharge. Learning to relax can help reduce stress and improve your state of mind. A healthy lifestyle is all about balance. Enjoy regular holidays, take time out on weekends to pamper and reward yourself, or simply rent a comedy DVD and laugh — it's wonderful medicine for the body and a great way to release stress. Massage is excellent for improving circulation and skin tone, and for relieving stress. Techniques such as deep breathing, yoga and meditation can help you focus on your goals and visualize what you want to achieve.

Don't forget about the importance of getting enough good-quality sleep. Studies have shown that people who don't get enough sleep are more likely to be overweight, so aim for seven to eight hours of good-quality sleep per night; it's one of the best things you can do for your body and your mind.

THE HEALTHY BODY

Losing fat

If you want to lose fat, you need to concentrate on three things:

You must burn more energy than you consume

Basically, if you eat more kilojoules (calories) than you require you'll gain weight, as all excess kilojoules can be converted into fat to be stored in the body. Most of us often eat a lot more than our body needs. I'm not one for counting every kilojoule, but it's important to always consider whether the food you are putting into your mouth is nutrient-dense or just empty kilojoules. By empty kilojoules, I mean food that contains little more than refined sugar and fat. This is true of foods like soft drinks, alcohol, pastries, chocolate, ice cream, fast foods, biscuits, sausages, processed meats, chips, doughnuts and cakes. A little pick here and there of the wrong foods doesn't seem like a lot, but it can often add up to quite a considerable amount in the course of a few weeks or months. Portion control is the key. Just by being aware of what you put into your mouth, you'll be able to control your food intake and still be able to enjoy your pleasures in moderation without compromising your diet.

You need to rev up your metabolism

The basal metabolic rate (BMR) is the amount of energy (kilojoules/calories) the body needs to maintain itself, which includes all the normal day-to-day bodily functions like breathing, digestion, circulation, temperature regulation and tissue repair. The metabolic rate is the speed with which the body burns these kilojoules. Some of us are born with fast and efficient metabolisms, while others have slower metabolic rates. BMR also drops as we age. This is mainly due to loss of hormone production, loss of skeletal muscle and a more sedentary lifestyle. Our BMR drops but our eating habits often stay the same — that's why many of us gain body fat in our thirties. The important thing to note is that no matter what your metabolic type, it can be controlled by what you eat and the lifestyle choices you make.

Eating a good breakfast is the first step to improving your metabolism. Your metabolic rate is higher in the mornings and tends to slow down in the late afternoon and evening, so it makes sense to consume most of your kilojoules at breakfast and lunch and not in one huge meal at night. That is one of the major factors in weight gain.

Exercise also plays a part. As you become fitter, a higher percentage of fat is used as fuel for the body. In particular, resistance or weight training improves metabolic rate, as it increases muscle mass, and the more muscle tissue you have in your body, the faster your metabolic rate.

You need to eat the right kind of foods for your activity level and lifestyle

This is about the importance of eating the right foods at the right time of day, suited to your energy needs and lifestyle. The recent phenomenon of low-carb diets causes much concern and confusion among most people wanting to lose weight. But a healthy diet should include good-quality carbohydrate, lean protein and essential fats. People should not eliminate carbohydrates from their diet. Rather, it is the quality of carbohydrate that is eaten and the time of day at which they are eaten that is important. Getting most of your vitamin-enriched carbohydrates from fresh fruit, vegetables and wholegrains, combined with lean protein and a little essential fat required by the body, is the basis of a good eating plan.

If we are trying to lose fat, we need to consider not only the amount of good carbohydrates we eat, but also the time of day we eat them. When we eat too many carbohydrates, the body burns them in preference to fat, and consequently fat-burning is not activated and weight loss becomes difficult. If the right carbohydrates are eaten at the right time of day and you supply your body with enough healthy food, then your body will allow fat to be burnt. So, eat most of your good carbs with a little protein during the day, at breakfast and lunch when you are most active, and unless you are running marathons or playing professional sport, dinner should instead focus on a healthy mix of water-based, high-fibre, lower-carbohydrate vegetables and lean protein. It's all a matter of balance. A lack of carbohydrate may lead to fatigue, tiredness and poor concentration. On the other hand, an excess of carbohydrates can be stored as body fat if not used up by the body.

The worst way to try to lose body fat is to starve yourself. When you do that, your body fights back by lowering your metabolic rate, increasing muscle-burning and decreasing fat-burning. In other words, muscle not fat is the first to go. The body thinks it hasn't enough food to survive, so it hangs on to its fat stores and in some cases even burns off protein.

So, a combination of aerobic exercise (cardio), which helps burn body fat and maintain cardiovascular fitness, combined with regular resistance training and good eating habits is the best combination to generate fat loss. You'll start burning body fat, increase your metabolism and, by eating regular meals, you won't feel the urge to binge at night when relaxing in front of the television.

Diet is a very personal thing and each person needs to get in tune with their body. Each person is different, and the health of the body depends on so many factors like body type, weight, activity, lifestyle, age, genetics, climate and work. However, the amount of energy needed by the body depends largely on the activity level of the individual. People with low activity levels need much less energy from food than people who are very active. For example, an office worker who did minimal exercise would need much less energy than an office worker who ran 10 km (6 miles) every day. Once we come to be in tune with our own body and its needs we can create a harmonious relationship within ourselves and in our day-to-day life. Eating good nutritious food and being active will then become a habit for life.

CREATING THE RIGHT FAT-LOSS ENVIRONMENT

Every day, repeat the following to yourself:

Yes I can! Yes I can! Yes I can!

A positive attitude is essential — not only in relation to fat loss, but in all aspects of life. So, no more negative thoughts … you can do anything.

To lose fat you must create the right fat-loss environment. Do your own kitchen audit — throw out all the junk food, packets of chips, processed foods and cereal boxes filled with nothing more than air and sugar. If you keep your kitchen free of junk you'll be less likely to eat junk. Fill your refrigerator and pantry with good, nutritious food. Include healthy snacks such as raw nuts and seeds, yoghurt and fresh fruits such as crisp apples, pears and juicy oranges.

Losing weight

It's frightening how many people are obsessed with weight when they go on a diet. They step on the scales every morning hoping to see some miraculous weight loss that has happened overnight. Only weigh yourself once a week and not every day. Aim for a weight loss of around 0.5–1 kg (1 lb 2 oz–2 lb 4 oz) a week, but that will vary with the individual. If you don't lose weight within the first few weeks, don't panic. Just keep going with all the hard work. Your body will soon let go of the fat if you stick with your regime.

It's also important for you to realize that weight by itself is not a good indication of fat loss. Weight doesn't take into account lean body mass due to lean muscle tissue, bones, vital organs and fluids. In fact, muscle weighs approximately four times more than fat! It's quite common for many people to lose fat and become leaner but not see much change when they jump on the scales, especially if they're exercising most days. The reason for this is that the fat loss is cancelled out by muscle gain. The scales won't register the change, but they'll definitely see it in how loosely their clothes fit and how their body shape changes.

For most of us, the best indications of fat loss are our clothes and the mirror we look in every morning. If you follow the 80/20 diet, you'll definitely see a change in how your clothes fit and improvements in how you look and feel. Just remember, fat loss takes time. The minimum amount of time to see results in most of us is about 12 weeks, and by that time your diet and exercise plan will have become a habit for life. So keep going — you're looking good!

Points to remember

- If you eat more kilojoules (calories) than you burn, you'll gain weight, as all kilojoules can be converted into fat if they are not used in the body for energy.
- You can help the body burn more fat by eating regularly and by eating the right kinds of foods at the right time of day.
- Always, always eat a good breakfast! It kick-starts the metabolism into action, setting you in power mode for the rest of the day. It also prevents you from overeating at night when you're more susceptible to cravings.
- Limit your high-fat foods and instead consume small amounts of essential fatty acids (EFAs), which are needed for optimal functioning of the body. These are contained in oily fish, raw nuts, seeds and avocado.
- Eat vegetables and salad with your lunch and evening meals. As part of the 80/20 diet you can eat unlimited green leafy vegetables and salads. Use appropriate home-made dressings such as 1–2 teaspoons linseed oil mixed with a little citrus juice or balsamic vinegar.
- Reduce your intake of refined carbohydrates, which include alcohol, sugar, white flour, white bread, biscuits, doughnuts, lollies, cakes and chips. Make these your 20 per cent, once-a-week foods.
- Eat regular amounts of good-quality lean protein to repair muscle tissue and maintain every cell in your body. Include at least three fish meals per week to get your quota of omega 3 fatty acids. If you're vegetarian, make sure to regularly consume vegetarian sources of protein and include linseeds (flax seeds) or a little linseed oil to get your omega 3 fatty acids.
- Increase your metabolic rate by eating regular healthy small meals throughout the day and by doing regular exercise. A combination of cardio and resistance training works best.
- Drink at least 2 litres (70 fl oz/8 glasses) pure water daily and keep coffee intake to no more than two cups. Try replacing your coffee with green tea, which helps to metabolize body fat.
- Think before you eat. Every time you're about to surrender to a fast-food hamburger, devour a pizza or scoff down a couple of doughnuts, ask yourself, 'Do I really want this fat to be part of my cells tomorrow?'
- Don't overeat late at night before going to bed. It's a recipe for fat gain!
- If you train hard but eat badly, you'll barely see a difference in your body shape. If you eat good, clean foods and train hard your body will thank you by shedding fat and making you trim, taut and terrific!

Imagine your body is like an expensive luxury car or a top-of-the-line sports car. You wouldn't just fill it up with regular fuel and forget the service and maintenance; you would use premium fuel and give the car a regular service and the best of everything to keep it running to peak performance. Well, looking after your body and health should be exactly the same. Keeping your body tuned up and in tip-top shape should be your primary goal.

Nutrition basics

This section explains the basics of nutrition. You'll find out what are the best proteins, fats and carbohydrates to eat and cook with, as well as gain useful information on fibre, vitamins, minerals, and food allergies and intolerances.

The nutrients in your body come from carbohydrate, protein, fat, fibre, water, vitamins and minerals. In nearly all cases, they must be obtained from the food we eat and drink. So making sure we eat a wide variety of foods and preparing them properly and simply is the key to long-term weight loss and to feeling great.

The fat-burning triangle

This pyramid illustrates the hierarchy of foods used in the 80/20 diet. Remember, too, that exercise and adequate rest are also essential parts of the plan.

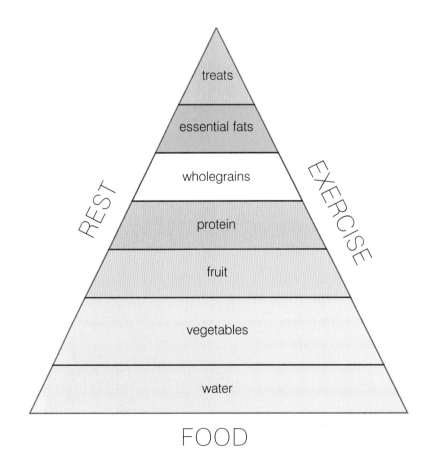

What is protein?

OUR BODY NEEDS PROTEIN to provide us with the amino acids needed by the body to build and repair muscle tissue, fight disease, protect skin, hair and nails, help maintain the correct pH balance in our cells and tissues, help maintain optimal fluid balance in body tissues, provide us with energy, make hormones and enable our cells to maintain and repair themselves.

Amino acids are divided into two types: non-essential and essential amino acids. Non-essential amino acids can be manufactured in the body, but the essential ones can only be obtained from the foods we eat — specifically from protein. The eight essential amino acids that we must obtain from our diet are isoleucine, leucine, lysine, methionine, phenylalanine, threonine, tryptophan and valine.

Protein is also divided into two categories. First-class proteins, or complete proteins, contain all the essential amino acids our body needs and include all animal sources of protein, as well as soya beans and quinoa, which are the only complete vegetable sources of protein. Good sources of complete protein are fish and shellfish, lean chicken, beef, veal, lamb, venison, pork, egg whites, cottage cheese, low-fat yoghurt and low-fat milk and soya milk, quinoa, tofu, soya beans, tempeh, whey and soya protein powder.

All vegetable sources of protein — with the exception of soya beans and quinoa, the supergrain — are called second-class proteins, as they contain only a few of the essential amino acids. They must be combined with other proteins to form a complete protein. For example, a meal might combine beans or lentils with steamed brown rice, or hummus spread onto wholegrain bread, or muesli with low-fat milk or soya milk to form complete proteins. Vegans must make sure they eat a wide variety of wholegrains, seeds, nuts, beans and legumes to get enough protein in their diet. Quinoa and soy should be a part of your weekly meal plan; substitute them accordingly in recipes.

Good sources of vegetable protein include soya beans, tofu, tempeh, soya milk, pot barley, puffed amaranth, quinoa, buckwheat, millet, couscous, spelt, nuts, and beans and pulses such as black-eyed peas, black beans, lentils, red kidney beans, adzuki beans, cannellini beans, broad (fava) beans, borlotti (cranberry) beans, peas and baked beans.

Don't go overboard, however. Too much protein can overwork the kidneys, cause high blood pressure and deplete the body of minerals, causing osteoporosis. Moderation is the key and your required amount depends on your age, weight and activity level. Usually 0.75–1 g times your body weight in kilograms will give you a good base indication of what you need. Pregnant and breastfeeding women, athletes and body builders will need slightly more, so it is best to discuss this with a dietician or nutritionist. Try to eat at least 2–3 protein-rich foods a day.

Limit intake of fatty proteins like sausages, salami, chorizo, fatty bacon and most processed deli meats, deep-fried chicken and fish, hamburgers, meat pies, sausage rolls, pâté, cheese, cream and full-fat milk.

What are carbohydrates?

CARBOHYDRATES are the preferred energy source for the body. As discussed, people should not eliminate carbohydrates completely from their diet in an effort to lose weight. What is important is the quality of the carbohydrate that is eaten and the time of day it is eaten (that is, what effect will it have on metabolism?). Getting most of our carbohydrates from vitamin-rich vegetables and fruit is the basis of a sustainable healthy eating plan, as these will provide the body with fantastic doses of low-fat energy and nutrients. Other good sources of good carbohydrates are beans, legumes and wholegrains.

Eating less refined sugar and fewer flour products, such as sweets, cakes, biscuits, white bread and pasta, will mean that the body will start to burn fat as the carbohydrate supply is limited. In the recipes in this book, I've included plenty of good-quality low glycemic index (GI) carbohydrates for all of my breakfast, lunch and dinner meals. The good carbohydrates are found in fruits and vegetables and some wholegrains, beans and legumes. The recipes contain few starchy, high-kilojoule (calorie) carbohydrates such as pasta, bread, potatoes and noodles, because so many of us tend to fill up our plates with these and never even get to the healthier vegetables, salads and proteins needed for wellbeing. Now, I'm not saying not to have them, I'm just saying that if you need to lose weight, you need to eat these in moderation, remembering portion control, and not to make them the major part of your meal.

What are fats?

SATURATED AND UNSATURATED FATS are terms most of us are all too familiar with. Briefly, unsaturated fats, which include monounsaturated and polyunsaturated fats, are usually liquid at room temperature and are derived from plant sources like avocado, olives and olive oils, oily fish, nuts and seeds and their oils. These are the fats the body needs in small quantities. Saturated fats are derived from animal sources, with the exception of palm oil and coconut oil, and are usually solid at room temperature. These are the fats to be avoided, or at least minimized.

Your body needs two essential fatty acids for optimal health and these can only be obtained from the foods we eat. They are linoleic acid (called omega 6) and alpha-linolenic acid (called omega 3), both forms of unsaturated fats. They are found in nuts and seeds such as linseeds (flax seeds), pumpkin seeds, sesame seeds, walnuts, almonds, cashew nuts, brazil nuts, pine nuts, hazelnuts, and also from soya beans and oily fish such as salmon, tuna, sardines, mackerel and herring. Small amounts of these unsaturated fats provide the body with the essential fatty acids vital for normal growth, repair, immunity, healthy skin, hormone balance and general wellbeing.

Finally, all fat is very kilojoule dense, so only small amounts are needed. Most of us consume way too much.

Foods to avoid are those that are high in saturated fats. They include things like suet, butter, lard, mascarpone cheese, full-fat cream cheese, cream, full-fat cheeses such as cheddar and stilton, chocolate, fatty bacon, fried foods, biscuits, crackers, and pastries such as brioche, croissants, pies, sausage rolls and shortcrust pastry. Saturated fats are notorious for raising 'bad' blood cholesterol levels and increasing the chance of blood clots and thrombosis, which can lead to blockage of the arteries.

One last type of fat to be aware of is trans fats, which are generally formed when unsaturated fats are processed to become hard at room temperature. Examples include some margarines and vegetable shortening, as well as fast foods and commercially baked goods that rely on these shortenings for a longer shelf life. Trans fats act like saturated fats in the body, so should be avoided. Generally, the softer or more liquid the fat is at room temperature, the less trans fat it contains and therefore the healthier it will be. So, as a general rule, eat fewer saturated and trans fats, and consume small amounts of healthy monounsaturated and polyunsaturated fats and you'll be on the right track.

In the kitchen, most oils are suited to certain preparations and cooking techniques over others. For example, for cooking such as sautéing, braising, baking or stir-frying, use oils such as olive, canola, grape seed, avocado, safflower, peanut or macadamia nut oil. For dressings, use polyunsaturated nut and seed oils such as linseed, walnut or virgin olive oil. Store these oils (except olive) in the refrigerator and away from bright light to keep them fresh.

What is fibre?

FIBRE IS FOUND NATURALLY only in plant foods. It consists of complex carbohydrate compounds that cannot be broken down by the body, but instead pass straight through our digestive system, creating bulk to help rid the body of waste. There are two types of fibre: insoluble and soluble. Most plant foods contain both types in varying proportions. Insoluble fibre speeds up movement in the intestinal tract by creating bulk, and is useful for treating digestive symptoms like irritable bowel syndrome and providing protection against certain cancers. Good sources of insoluble fibre are grains, vegetables and pulses, such as wheat bran, barley, rice, broccoli, carrots, beans and lentils. Soluble fibre is known to lower bad LDL blood cholesterol. It is found in citrus fruits, apples and pears, the plant psyllium, oats, barley and rye, beans and pulses like lentils, kidney beans and soya beans. In addition, both types of fibre are great for controlling blood sugar levels by slowing the absorption of glucose into the blood stream.

An increase in your fibre intake should be coupled with an increase in water intake, as fibre absorbs a lot of liquid. Without enough water, too much fibre will actually clog you up.

Important vitamins and minerals

When vitamins and minerals are discussed, many people think about them in tablet form. But here I'll outline what vitamins and minerals are contained in the various foods we eat, as well as discuss some important terms. It is helpful to know where to find the nutrients your body requires so that you can tailor your diet to suit your individual needs.

Vitamins enable proteins, fats and carbohydrates to function as a synchronized unit, providing the body with energy, strength and good health. Vitamins are either fat-soluble or water-soluble. The fat-soluble vitamins are A, D, E and K. These vitamins can be stored within the fat deposits of the body and within the liver. Note, however, that fat-soluble vitamins, when taken in large amounts, can become toxic. Water-soluble vitamins include vitamin C and the B vitamins. These vitamins need to be replenished on a regular basis as any excess is excreted in the urine.

Minerals are divided into two categories: major minerals, which include calcium, chloride, magnesium, phosphorus, potassium, sodium and sulphur; and trace minerals, which include chromium, copper, fluorine, iodine, iron, manganese, selenium and zinc. The body contains only small reserves of minerals and deficiency can result in health problems, including anaemia (iron), osteoporosis (calcium) and a week immune system (zinc).

Antioxidants are compounds that protect us from disease and illness. They help to strengthen our immune system and fight free radicals that cause disease, ageing and molecular breakdown within our cells. The principal antioxidants are vitamins C, E and A, coenzyme Q10, zinc, selenium and glutathione. Each one seems to work in a different way to counteract free radical damage, so they're all important.

Free radicals are formed during normal metabolism in the body or by outside factors such as pollution, X-rays, poor diet, smoking and ultra-violet radiation and have been linked to the development of cancer and disease. As free radical levels rise, so does the need for additional antioxidants. Smokers, for example, need two to three times as much vitamin C to achieve the same antioxidant blood levels as non-smokers. You can normally tell the antioxidant value of a food by its intense colour or strong smell. So, if you want a lean, healthy body, radiant skin and less wrinkles, make it a daily ritual to fill up on antioxidant-rich foods such as broccoli, cabbage, garlic, carrots, onions, berries, oily fish and brussels sprouts.

Some of the main players

VITAMIN A — This antioxidant vitamin is essential for good eyesight and for maintaining healthy skin and hair. It can help neutralize free radicals in the body, reducing their damaging effects on the cells. Many plants are high in betacarotene, which is converted by the body into vitamin A. Good sources are all red, yellow and green vegetables, including raw carrots, tomatoes, sweet potato, red capsicum (pepper), cabbage, broccoli, lettuce, English spinach, peas, brussels sprouts and chilli. Remember, the richer the colour, the richer the nutritional value. Fruit sources include all orange-fleshed fruits such as mango, rockmelon, papaya and fresh and dried apricots.

B VITAMINS — These are a group of eight water-soluble vitamins that work together in the body, though each one has a different role to play. Generally, they are essential for growth and proper development of the nervous system, the healthy digestion of food, and bodily maintenance and metabolism. The B vitamins include folate B9 (folic acid), which interacts with vitamin B12 in the synthesis of DNA. This is very important for pregnant women to know, as these vitamins can help prevent birth defects such as spina bifida. Deficiency of folic acid has been linked to anemia, poor growth, fatigue, depression and heart disease.

As the B vitamins are water soluble, they need to be replenished daily. Good food sources are lamb's liver, seaweed, turkey and chicken, wholegrains such as wheat germ and rolled (porridge) oats, sunflower seeds, nuts, eggs, shiitake mushrooms, oily fish, pulses, fortified breakfast cereals, baby sweet corn, brussels sprouts, oranges, asparagus, brown rice and leafy green vegetables. Note, however, that the B vitamins are lost if food is stored for too long, or is cooked excessively. Consume the food as soon as possible after purchasing, and use quick cooking methods such as stir-frying, steaming and braising.

VITAMIN C — This water-soluble vitamin is essential for so many aspects of good health, from the maintenance of red blood cells to warding off colds. It's a powerful antioxidant, helps maintain a healthy immune system and is good for the skin, as it assists in the formation of collagen, a component of the skin, bones and connective tissues.

Like the B vitamins, this vitamin is destroyed during cooking and long storing, so eat fruit raw, and try eating vegetables raw or just very lightly cooked, such as by stir-frying or light steaming. Do not boil vegetables because the vitamins will leach out into the water. Good sources of vitamin C are all types of fruits, especially apples, pears, citrus (oranges, grapefruit, mandarins), blackcurrants, blueberries, kiwi fruit, strawberries, watermelon, rockmelon, mango, papaya, red grapes, dark plums and red cherries. Vegetables include red, yellow and green capsicum (pepper), red and green chillies, broccoli, brussels sprouts, green and red cabbage, and lettuce.

VITAMIN D — This fat-soluble vitamin is essential for bone growth and mineral balance in the body. Just 30 minutes of sunlight a day enables the skin to make vitamin D. Food sources of vitamin D are eggs, cod liver oil and oily fish like salmon, herring, sardines, trout, tuna and mackerel.

VITAMIN E — This powerful antioxidant helps slow down premature cellular ageing, prevents the cell membranes from damage, prevents the build-up of plaque in the arteries, and helps thin the blood. Good food sources are wheat germ, sunflower seeds, nuts (such as almonds, hazelnuts, pine nuts and brazil nuts), nut oils, avocado, tomato, sweet potato, English spinach and oily fish like salmon, tuna and sardines.

GLUTATHIONE — Your body makes this powerful antioxidant from the non-essential amino acids l-cystine, glutamic acid and l-glycine, which come from eating protein. Without glutathione, your body would collapse from uncontrolled oxidation, and you would have little resistance to bacteria, viruses and cancer. Glutathione levels decrease as we grow older, and also as a result of stress, illness, fatigue and over-exercising. It's important to eat at least 2–3 serves of protein a day to maintain good levels of glutathione in the body and a healthy immune system.

COENZYME Q10 — Another powerful antioxidant, coenzyme Q10 helps the body convert food to energy, strengthens the heart, helps to maintain a healthy immune system and slows ageing. Deficiency has been linked with heart problems including arrhythmia, angina and high blood pressure. Good sources are fish, meat, vegetable oils, wheat germ, rice bran, beans, English spinach and broccoli.

CALCIUM — This mineral is needed throughout your entire life. It is vital not only in ensuring that correct bone mass is reached in childhood years, but also in preventing osteoporosis in later life. It is also essential for the proper functioning of muscles and nerves, and works closely with magnesium in maintaining healthy bones. (Magnesium acts to increase calcium absorption from the diet and calcium retention in the bones.) Absorption of calcium is aided by getting adequate amounts of vitamin D and essential fatty acids, along with regular exercise, which can stimulate the growth of new bone cells. Conversely, high-fibre foods, excess alcohol and the tannin in tea and coffee can affect absorption. Good sources include dairy products, dark green leafy vegetables and sea vegetables, tofu, sardines and salmon (including their bones), nuts like almonds and brazil nuts, wholegrains, sesame seeds, soya beans, dried figs, chickpeas, prawns (shrimp), cabbage, broccoli and seaweed.

CHROMIUM — This trace element helps control blood glucose levels and regulate the metabolism of fats and carbohydrates. A diet high in sugar depletes the body's store of chromium. Good sources are beef, liver, chicken, oysters, eggs, wheat germ, capsicum (pepper), apples, bananas, English spinach, black pepper and molasses.

IRON — The main function of this trace mineral is to carry oxygen in the blood to the cells throughout the body. Iron can also increase the body's resistance to infection and help the healing process. Iron deficiency is a particular concern among individuals, especially women, who are extremely active or on low-kilojoule or vegetarian diets. They need to be regularly tested to ensure they are not iron deficient. Iron from animal sources is more easily absorbed into the body from the intestine than iron from plant foods. Vitamin C can aid the absorption of iron, so it's a good idea to eat a piece of grilled (broiled) beef along with some stir-fried broccoli or have a glass of orange juice with your wholegrain cereal at breakfast. Good sources are fortified cereals, seaweed, sesame and pepitas (pumpkin seeds), nuts, beans and pulses (lentils, soya beans and red kidney beans), lean red meat, dried peaches and apricots, English spinach, silverbeet (Swiss chard), broccoli, leafy greens, eggs, brown rice, barley and couscous.

MAGNESIUM — This mineral is essential for the metabolism of glucose for fuel, muscle and nerve function, the regulation of temperature and to work with calcium to maintain strong healthy bones. Evidence suggests it has a strong role to play in helping prevent osteoporosis. Absorption is affected by heavy alcohol consumption. Good sources are wholegrains, nuts, seeds and green vegetables.

SELENIUM — Selenium is an important trace mineral and powerful antioxidant that helps protect us from heart disease, some cancers and premature ageing. Research suggests it increases the effectiveness of vitamin E, and is important in maintaining a healthy immune system, normal growth, fertility, thyroid action and healthy skin and hair. Good food sources include seafood such as squid, tuna, sardines, salmon, cod, prawns (shrimp), swordfish and mussels, as well as lean pork, wholegrains, seeds, brazil nuts and walnuts, raisins, mushrooms and lentils.

ZINC — This super trace mineral is essential for normal growth, development, fertility, healthy skin, hair and nails, a healthy immune system, the healing of wounds and destroying free radicals. It's found in meat, crabs and oysters, dairy products, wholegrains such as wheat germ, pulses, pine nuts, cashews and pecans, poppy seeds, pumpkin seeds (pepitas), sesame seeds, sunflower seeds, seaweed and cocoa powder.

Food intolerances and diabetes

Each week I receive emails from people asking me to design recipes to cater for their specific dietary needs. In the recipe section of this book, you'll find lots of recipes for breakfast, lunch and dinner, to enjoy as part of the 80/20 diet. Many recipes can be altered to suit individual tastes and special dietary requirements. The brief outline below of dietary dilemmas will assist you when making food choices, but always check with your doctor or other health professional if in doubt about what you can or can't eat.

GLUTEN INTOLERANCE — Gluten is a protein found in cereals, in particular wheat, but also rye, barley, oats and triticale. Intolerance to gluten can lead to coeliac disease, a painful condition that damages the lining of the small intestine, preventing the absorption of food. If you are allergic to or intolerant of gluten you are often very restricted in what you can eat, as gluten is present in so many foods. Obvious culprits are breads, cereals and pastas but many processed foods can contain gluten — reading the labels when purchasing food is essential. Local coeliac societies provide detailed lists of gluten-free foods.

LACTOSE INTOLERANCE — This is the inability to properly digest a sugar called lactose, found in dairy products such as milk, soft cheese and cream. The intolerance is caused by the absence of an enzyme called lactase, which breaks down lactose. Symptoms include gas and bloating. Each person's sensitivity is different, but with the help of a health professional, sufferers usually learn how much lactose they can tolerate before the body starts to react.

If avoiding lactose products, such as milk and dairy, it is important to eat other calcium-rich foods such as sardines and tinned salmon in spring water (including the bones), seaweed (kombu or nori), seeds and nuts, cabbage and broccoli. Yoghurt containing live cultures can be eaten, as the bacteria in the yoghurt digests the milk sugar for you. Yoghurt also provides calcium, iron, phosphorus and potassium. Plain yoghurt is better than flavoured yoghurt.

WHEAT INTOLERANCE — When diagnosed, wheat intolerance is often treated by simply eliminating wheat from the diet. Common symptoms such as bloating, headaches and loose stools often go immediately once the diet is adjusted. Like those suffering gluten intolerance, careful reading of food labels is vital.

DIABETES — This serious condition can cause heart disease, stroke, blindness, nerve damage, kidney problems and gum disease. There are two types. Type 1 diabetes is when the body does not make insulin, requiring people with type 1 to take insulin every day. Type 2 diabetes is when the body does not make or use insulin well. People with type 2 can often control their diabetes with diet, weight management and some medication. To manage diabetes, it's important to eat regular portions of fresh vegetables and fruit, fish, lean meats, beans, wholegrains and low-fat dairy products — basically, all the foods that contain complex carbohydrates, fibre, protein and essential fatty acids. If diabetic, you should eat fewer foods high in fats and refined sugar such as take-aways, highly processed foods and alcohol. To help blood sugar levels it's also important to consume regular small meals and snacks that are low- to medium-GI and high in fibre. Eat foods such as oats, beans, almonds, apples and pears. Diabetics should also get at least 30–60 minutes of exercise every day and try to maintain a healthy weight.

The superfoods: seasonal fruits and vegetables

In order to feel full of energy and ready to take on the world every day, we need to focus on what sort of fuel we're putting into our bodies. Fruits and vegetables are the five-star foods in this regard because of their special abilities to promote and sustain good health. They naturally provide us with so many vitamins, minerals and nutrients, as well as the all-important phytochemicals. These are chemical compounds present in all plant foods ('phyto' meaning plant). Research suggests they are instrumental in boosting the immune system and fighting cardiovascular disease, diabetes, insulin insensitivity and obesity. Phytochemicals are responsible for a plant's colour, flavour and odour. So, when shopping, select brightly coloured, seasonal, fruits and vegetables. It's also important to eat a wide variety of fruit and vegetables, as each one contains slightly different protective substances, which all contribute to overall health.

APPLES — These are a good source of vitamin C and both insoluble and soluble fibre (in the form of pectin). Apples are believed to help relieve constipation, lower cholesterol levels and prevent colon and other types of digestive cancer. The pectin can help control appetite by creating a feeling of fullness in the stomach, thus making you less likely to go hunting in the refrigerator for high-fat snacks. Apples also contain significant amounts of a mineral called boraon, which is known to help strengthen bones and maintain alertness.

Grate an apple into your next bowl of bircher muesli, or make a retro Waldorf salad by combining finely sliced apple, celery, walnuts and lean chicken breast, with a herb and honey mustard yoghurt dressing. Mix sliced apple with sugar-free apricot jam and then wrap it in filo pastry for a delicious low-fat apple strudel. Puréed apples can replace half the fat in cake and muffin mixes.

ARTICHOKE — The two common types are the globe and jerusalem artichokes. Though unrelated, both are good sources of vitamin C, thiamine, fibre, calcium, phosphorus, niacin and potassium. When selecting globe artichokes, choose ones with compact, heavy heads and avoid those with opened out, curled or dry looking leaves. Cooking time will depend on the size and age of the artichoke. Globe artichokes are delicious boiled, braised, stuffed or tossed into salads. Jerusalem artichokes should be treated in the same way as you would other tubers such as potato — for example, they taste fantastic roasted or mashed.

ASPARAGUS — These succulent spears contain folate, betacarotene (vitamin A in plants), vitamins C and E and fibre. They are a delicious food that suits simple preparations and uncomplicated flavours. They can be eaten hot or cold, tossed raw or cooked into salads, added to omelettes or served as a bed for freshly poached seafood or chicken. When buying, choose crisp, brightly coloured, straight specimens. It is not necessary to peel small, thin asparagus, but you may have to peel away any tough fibrous ends from the larger, thicker varieties. As well, because they are quite perishable, it is best to buy locally-grown asparagus and eat them within a few days of purchasing.

AVOCADOS — These fruits are high in fat, but much of it is the good monounsaturated type. They are also a great source of vitamins C, E and the B group, as well as potassium. I like to add avocado to many of my salads: try mixing chopped avocado with poached chicken or king prawns (shrimp), finishing off with chopped coriander (cilantro) leaves, spring onion (scallion) and a light dressing made from lime juice, fish sauce, honey, garlic and chilli. They also make fantastic healthy dressings and dips. Blend with a little lime juice, water, honey, garlic, sea salt and pepper for a delicious healthy dressing for chicken, seafood and leafy salads.

BANANA — This convenient fruit is a good source of fibre, vitamins (in particular vitamin C) and potassium and iron. Thread chopped banana onto skewers, then place in the freezer for an instant iced dessert. Coat in a little honey or melted chocolate and roll in crushed cashew nuts and coconut for a simple dessert. Don't forget to drizzle the chopped banana with a little lemon juice to prevent browning.

Add mashed banana to cakes as a substitute for half of the butter or oil. It will keep the cake moist without adding extra fat. Adding banana instead of egg to a cake mix is also a good idea for vegans or those who cannot eat eggs. They also add body and flavour to a nice icy protein shake.

Don't eat raw unripe bananas, as they contain resistant starch, which ferments in the intestine, causing wind. You can, however, use unripe bananas in cooking. Add to a pumpkin (winter squash), English spinach and coconut curry, or braise with lemon grass, coconut and makrut (kaffir) lime leaves and serve with steamed white fish and green vegetables.

BEANS — These are delicious eaten raw in fragrant Thai salads, lightly steamed with just a squeeze of lemon juice and a pinch of sea salt, or quickly stir-fried with a little soy sauce, mirin and toasted cashew nuts. Choose young, firm, straight pods with good colour. They should snap crisply when broken. Beans are a good source of the antioxidants betacarotene and vitamin C, as well as fibre.

BEETROOT (BEETS) — This ruby-coloured vegetable is a good source of dietary fibre, folic acid, potassium, magnesium and vitamin C. The juice is thought to aid kidney function, and the leafy stalks provide betacarotene, calcium and iron. Beetroot is delicious grated raw into salads, roasted, boiled or steamed. Combine with orange segments and throw into leafy salads, blend the juice with apple and carrot for a yummy detox energy tonic, and serve with red meats, chicken or turkey. To fully appreciate its sweet flavour, buy beetroot raw and not tinned. Do not peel before cooking and be careful when removing the skin once cooked so as not to stain clothes or cutting boards. The leafy green stalks can be used in the same way as English spinach or silver beet (Swiss chard).

BERRIES (blackberries, blueberries, cranberries, raspberries and strawberries) — All berries contain a whopping amount of the antioxidant vitamin C, along with varying amounts of folate, iron and fibre. Both blueberries and cranberries are thought to be useful in the treatment of urinary tract infections. Berries are delicious in all sorts of salads and make yummy low-fat desserts and smoothies. Frozen berries can be processed with a little apple juice to make an instant sorbet, folded into muffin or pancake mixes or tossed into savoury salads.

BROCCOLI — This is an excellent source of the antioxidants vitamins C and E and betacarotene. It is also rich in folate and high in fibre. Broccoli is best eaten raw or lightly cooked. I like to make a raw broccoli salad by finely chopping broccoli and mixing it with chopped coriander (cilantro) leaves, spring onion (scallion), some pepitas (pumpkin seeds) and walnuts, then finishing off with a dressing made from tahini, lime juice, honey and miso.

BRUSSELS SPROUTS — An excellent source of vitamin C, fibre and folate, brussels sprouts are also extremely beneficial in fighting free radicals. Choose small compact heads with a good bright green colour. Brussels sprouts can be steamed, stir-fried or boiled, and if eating whole it is best to cut a shallow cross in the stem to ensure even cooking. Don't overcook, as a sulphur odour will develop, which some people find unappetizing.

CABBAGE — This vegetable contains similar anti-carcinogenic phytochemicals as broccoli and brussels sprouts, and is also a good source of vitamin C, betacarotene and folate. The dark green leaves contain most of the vitamins and minerals; the paler centre leaves contain much less. The juice is reputed to soothe indigestion, heal ulcers and relieve constipation. When selecting, choose cabbage with solid firm heads. The outer leaves should be strongly coloured and not limp. Cabbage can be shredded raw into salads such as coleslaws made with a little olive oil and lemon juice, stir-fried with garlic and chilli, steamed or braised with herbs and topped with a sprinkle of finely chopped walnuts. The leaves can be blanched and stuffed with assorted chopped vegetables, beans and brown rice. Cook quickly to retain maximum nutrition and flavour.

CAPSICUM (PEPPER) — This smooth, shiny fruit is available in many colours, with red, green and yellow being the most common. They are a good source of betacarotene, vitamin C and B6, although red capsicums are much richer than the other varieties in these vitamins. They all contain the natural painkiller capsaicin, clinically proven to be useful against arthritic pain. When buying, choose well-shaped, thick-walled, firm fruit with a uniform bright, glossy colour. They can be eaten raw in salads, tossed through stir-fries, roasted and made into pesto, stuffed with grated zucchini (courgette), English spinach and cottage cheese or ricotta, and added to thick tomato sauces and soups.

CARROTS — High in betacarotene, vitamins A and C, and a good source of dietary fibre, carrots are legendary in the fight against disease, including cancer, heart disease, strokes and cholesterol-related illnesses. Studies have shown that eating just 1–2 carrots a day can be instrumental in preventing ill health. Carrots are easy to incorporate into recipes. Add to a stock for a simple and creamy carrot soup, lightly steam and toss with honey and oven-roasted sesame seeds for a quick side dish, and grate and mix with tahini, miso, mirin and some seeds and nuts for a delicious, healthy salad.

CAULIFLOWER — Like cabbage and other members of the cruciferous family, cauliflower is a good source of the cancer-fighting agents known as glucosinolates. It is also a good source of vitamin C, fibre, folate and potassium. When selecting, look for firm, compact, white heads without spots or bruises. Cauliflower can be sliced thinly and added raw into salads, stir-fried, oven-roasted with a little olive oil and garlic, or steamed and puréed to make a low-carbohydrate mash or a delicious cauliflower soup, seasoned with a drizzle of pesto.

CELERY — Asian medicine has long used celery to lower blood pressure. It contains moderate amounts of vitamin C and is a good source of vitamin A, calcium, phosphorus, sodium, potassium and fibre. When buying, choose crisp, firm, well-coloured stalks with no blemishes or limp leaves. Celery adds a wonderful crisp texture to any salad — I like to add finely sliced celery to my poached chicken salad and mix with a dressing made from lemon juice, olive oil, curry powder and honey. Stir-fry celery quickly to retain its crisp texture.

CHERRIES — A good source of vitamin C, potassium and fibre, cherries are also valued for their ability to remove toxins and cleanse the kidneys. Choose cherries that are plump, firm and dark red in colour with a fresh green stem. Avoid small pale cherries, which are most likely immature and lacking in juice and flavour. Cherries are delicious on their own or tossed into crisp leafy salads and topped with chopped almonds or brazil nuts.

CHILLIES — Like capsicums (peppers), chillies contain high levels of capsaicin. The hotter the chilli, the more it contains. Capsaicin helps to lower blood pressure and regulate the heartbeat. It can also stimulate the metabolic rate and improve circulation by assisting the blood vessels to widen, thus letting more blood through. Capsaicin is also known to aid digestion and be a beneficial tonic for the lungs, as its peppery heat stimulates secretions that help clear a stuffed-up nose or congested lungs. Choose chillies with a good colour and a green stem. Less is more when adding chilli to dishes. Start with a little and add more, a bit at a time, until you reach the desired heat.

CITRUS FRUIT — Oranges, mandarins, grapefruit, lemons and limes have been called the complete package for natural anti-cancer agents. An excellent source of vitamin C, they help maintain the body's defence against bacterial infections. Citrus has a unique type of fibre that, in studies, appears to dramatically reduce cholesterol. Citrus is fantastic in all sorts of salads and makes the best low-fat dressings. Serve segments with crisp salad leaves, crunchy walnuts and sliced dates. Marinate lean lamb cutlets or steaks in a blend of lemon juice, garlic and cumin before grilling (broiling). Make an aromatic Thai salad dressing for chicken or seafood salads using a mixture of lime juice, fish sauce, honey, garlic and chilli. Mandarins make a great snack for kids as well as for adults, as they are easy to peel and taste delicious.

CORN — Simple is best when cooking with corn. I like mine steamed with a light sprinkle of sea salt, thrown into hot miso soup, or mixed with egg whites, coriander (cilantro) and a little rice flour for the best sweet corn fritters. These delicious cobs are a good source of vitamin C, fibre, thiamin (vitamin B1), pantothenic acid (vitamin B5) and folate. The fibre found in corn can help stabilize blood sugar levels and provide steady, slow-burning energy.

CUCUMBER — These refreshing vegetables are a good source of vitamin C, potassium, magnesium and dietary fibre. They have a high water content and are mildly diuretic. Research suggests that the phytochemicals in cucumber, called sterols (found mainly in the cucumber's skin), can also help to lower blood cholesterol. Choose firm, green specimens with no signs of yellow. Cucumbers are mostly eaten raw in salads, dips and dressings or added to stir-fries just before serving.

EGGPLANT (AUBERGINE) — This shiny purple vegetable can be baked, boiled, steamed or grilled (broiled). It is delicious in salads and makes a good substitute for pasta in lasagne. Try baking whole eggplants and blending the pulp with a little tahini and lemon juice for a delicious and healthy mayonnaise, dip or spread. Salting beforehand to remove bitterness is not really necessary these days due to modern varieties, but it does tend to reduce the amount of oil the eggplant will soak up during cooking. When selecting, choose eggplants that are firm and heavy for their size. Their colour should be rich purple with a fresh green stalk. They are very low in kilojoules (calories) and are a good source of dietary fibre and minerals.

ENGLISH SPINACH — This tops the list, along with other green leafy vegetables, of cancer-fighting foods. A super source of antioxidants, spinach is also high in folate. Serve alongside poached fish drizzled with lemon juice and linseed oil, or toss with aromatics such as lemon grass, chilli, lime juice and honey and mix with poached shredded chicken and oven-roasted cashew nuts. Or steam English spinach, drizzle it with a little soy sauce and mirin and eat as a warm salad.

FENNEL — In natural medicine, fennel is used to aid digestion and relieve constipation. Research also suggests that it can reduce the toxic effects of alcohol on the body. It contains vitamin C and iron. Choose firm, plump bulbs with fresh green stalks. Fennel is delicious chopped finely into salads and marries well with seafood and citrus.

FIGS — These are an excellent source of dietary fibre, as well as vitamin C and potassium. Choose fresh figs that have good colour for their variety and are plump and free from blemishes. The skin is quite thin, so there is no need to peel the fruit when serving. Figs are a great addition to a salad. They can be eaten fresh, baked or stewed, and incorporated into cake, bread and muffin batters. Puréed dried figs make a good alternative to sweet jams.

GINGER — This knobbly rhizome stimulates the circulation and aids digestion. It is a well-known remedy for nausea, travel sickness, colds and flu. When selecting fresh ginger, choose heavy, smooth roots free from soft spots and wrinkles. Use grated fresh ginger in stir-fries, salads, Asian-style casseroles and marinades. It is delicious when folded through low-fat cakes and fruity puddings. Try blending a little ginger and ground cinnamon into low-fat banana smoothies or make an instant ginger ale by blending a piece of ginger with home-made lemonade.

GRAPES — Red and black grapes contain 20 known antioxidants that work together to fend off attacks by free radicals. The antioxidants are in the grape skin, so the more colourful the skin, the greater the amount of antioxidants you'll receive. Grapes make a fantastic natural sugar fix, so are ideal for those wanting to avoid temptation. Add to any fruit salad or mix into crisp green salads with a little shredded poached chicken and a handful of walnuts.

KALE — Part of the cabbage family, this wonderful vegetable is a good source of all three antioxidants: betacarotene and vitamins C and E. It is also rich in naturally occuring glucosinolates, which help in the fight against cancer. Select fresh, crisp leaves with no signs of wilting and straight crisp stalks. The leaves are delicious in soups and stir-fries, shredded and added raw to salads with citrus vinaigrette, or used as a wrap for grains and vegetables.

KIWI FRUIT — A great source of vitamin C, potassium and soluble fibre. It also contains the mineral chromium, which is useful in the management of diabetes and the metabolism of fat. The whole kiwi fruit including the skin is edible, but most people prefer to discard the skin. Slice and add to a green salad with poached chicken and a orange pecan dressing or make a yummy smoothie with honeydew melon, pineapple and mint.

LEEKS — These are a great source of vitamin C, fibre and iron. Before using, make sure to trim away the root and the tough green leaves. Cut in half and wash well in water. Use as a flavour base in pies and soups, sauté with mushrooms and fold into an omelette, or add to roasted capsicums (peppers) and drizzle with balsamic vinegar.

LETTUCE — These leaves are very low in kilojoules and are a useful source of vitamins, minerals, iron and fibre. The darker the leaves the more vitamins and iron they contain. Varieties include sweet and crunchy iceberg and cos (romaine), mild and moreish butter lettuce, peppery watercress and rocket (arugula), and the slightly bitter ruby-coloured radicchio. All these leaves can be enjoyed with just a simple dressing of lemon juice and olive oil, or made into delectable meals by tossing with tender strips of poached chicken or seafood and fresh garden herbs.

MANGO — This glorious fruit is loaded with vitamins A, C and E and soluble fibre. Select mangoes that are free of bruises. Ripe fruit will yield to gentle pressure and have a wonderful sweet aroma. Sliced mango cheeks are best eaten fresh. They complement seafood and chicken and add richness to low-fat drinks, cakes and preserves. They look pretty sliced over leafy green salads and make terrific salsas when mixed with a little sweet chilli sauce and lime.

MELONS — These beauties are low in kilojoules — great for those watching their weight. Rockmelons (or any orange-fleshed melon) contain good amounts of betacarotene, vitamin C and potassium. Watermelon is high in vitamins A and C, as well as being a very concentrated source of the powerful antioxidant lycopene. Honeydew is high in folic acid and iron. The porous skin of rockmelon allows the sweet aroma to come through, so fragrance is the best indication of ripeness. When choosing honeydew melon, look for deep gold or pale green-white skin. Watermelons should feel heavy and full. Melons are an ideal fruit to serve chilled as a refreshing dessert: cut into chunks and serve in a hollowed-out watermelon, make into sorbets and granitas, and add to punches and cocktails. Rockmelons make a fantastic breakfast when topped with blueberries, roasted cashew nuts and a dollop of yoghurt.

MUSHROOMS (BUTTON, FIELD, OYSTER, SHIITAKE, SWISS BROWN) — These are very low in carbohydrates and a good source of B vitamins, folic acid and protein. Shiitake mushrooms contain chemicals that help fight cancer. Eat raw in salads with a light drizzle of balsamic vinegar, lemon juice, or soy sauce and sesame oil. Or use large field mushrooms as low-fat pizza bases instead of dough and top with English spinach, ricotta and pine nuts.

OKRA — This little vegetable is a good source of vitamin C, betacarotene, folic acid and soluble fibre. It also contains various minerals including magnesium. It has good thickening properties and can be used in soups and casseroles as an alternative to flour. Okra goes well with other vegetables such as tomato, onion, eggplant (aubergine), corn and capsicum (pepper).

ONIONS AND GARLIC — These powerful agents of good health are linked with everything from helping to prevent cancer and blood clots to raising levels of good cholesterol and lowering blood pressure. They also have anti-bacterial and anti-inflammatory properties that help keep colds and flu at bay. Onions and garlic are fantastic in salads, soups, hearty low-fat casseroles and stir-fries.

PAPAYA — This golden fruit is so nutritionally rich that it is known as the medicine tree in Africa and the Caribbean. The enzyme papain is extracted from papaya, and is beneficial for those with digestive problems. Shredded green papaya makes a lovely Thai salad when combined with lime juice, fish sauce, chilli and a little honey. This fruit is best eaten fresh and simply prepared: top it with passionfruit for breakfast, toss in salads with a little citrus for tang, and use the purée in smoothies. Ripen green papaya at room temperature and then store in the refrigerator.

PARSNIPS — Related to carrots, celery and parsley, parsnips are a good source of fibre, folic acid, iron and vitamin C. Before using, make sure to scrub well and trim the top root. In your next mash, use half potato and half parsnip, add parsnips to soups and slow-cooked casseroles, or roast them with a little olive oil, rosemary, garlic and sea salt.

PASSIONFRUIT — This tropical fruit is a great source of vitamin C, B3 and dietary fibre. It is delicious eaten straight from the skin or folded into low-fat ice creams, sorbets and low-fat cakes. Mix a little pulp through chilled lemonade or apple juice to add extra zing and vitamins, or marry with papaya and mango for a refreshing fruit salad. Passionfruit also makes a lovely addition to a summery chicken salad.

PEARS — These well-loved fruits are a quick and convenient source of energy. Pears contain vitamins C and B2 and potassium, which is essential for muscle contraction, and therefore proper heart function. Pears are also a good source of the dietary fibre pectin, which is helpful in regulating cholesterol and controlling blood sugar levels. The ripe fruit is sweet and juicy with a lovely buttery texture. Grate into your morning bowl of muesli, toss through salads with lean sliced chicken breast, and poach in red wine, spiced with cinnamon.

PEAS — These little green balls of goodness are a good source of fibre, vitamins and minerals. They are delicious added to soups and salads, mashed with a little garlic, black pepper, lemon and avocado, or puréed into a creamy soup with chicken or vegetable stock.

PERSIMMON — These fruits are available late summer and throughout autumn. Looking a bit like an orange tomato, they are a great source of vitamins A and C. Choose firm, glossy fruit that is plump and free of blemishes. I prefer non-astringent varieties like Fuyu, Izu, Maekawa, Jiro, Matsumoto or Wase Fuyu. Persimmons can be eaten on their own, or, like most fruit, added to fruit salads. Chop the flesh and mix with coriander (cilantro) leaves and sweet chilli sauce for an easy salsa to go over grilled (broiled) or barbecued snapper or king prawns (shrimp).

PINEAPPLE — A good source of vitamin C, pineapples also contain the enzyme bromelain, which helps digestion by aiding the breakdown of protein. Pineapples do not ripen after harvesting, so choose ones that have a fresh, sweet smell and at least one-third of the skin golden in colour. Toss juicy pineapple through salads, use on kebabs and make into sweet salsas. They go well with lean, tender chicken or freshly cooked seafood. The juice is sensational in all sorts of punches and sorbets.

POTATO — These are a good source of vitamin C, fibre, potassium, magnesium, niacin and thiamine. Make sure to remove any green bits on the skin as they are poisonous. Potatoes have lots of uses: make a batch of low-fat chips by cutting them into wedges and spraying them with a little olive oil, then seasoning with rosemary, garlic and black pepper. Roast in a preheated oven at 220°C (425°F/Gas 7) for 40 minutes until golden and crisp. Mash potatoes with low-fat milk and a little roasted garlic instead of butter and cream. Make superb fish patties by mixing cooked potatoes with fresh herbs, peas, chopped avocado and a tin of salmon, then form into patties and coat in wholemeal (whole-wheat) breadcrumbs, ground almonds or wheat germ. Sauté until golden on both sides or bake in a hot oven until golden. Make a warm potato salad by steaming a batch of kipfler (fingerling) or new potatoes until tender, then cut in half and combine with sliced spring onion (scallion), chopped coriander (cilantro) leaves, mint and peas. Make a dressing with lime juice, low-fat coconut milk, fish sauce and sweet chilli sauce and mix through.

PRUNES — Dried plums are known as prunes. They have a laxative effect due to certain compounds that stimulate the bowel. Studies have shown that a regular intake reduces bad types of cholesterol in the blood, and they may also protect against colon cancer. Add prunes to Moroccan-style stews scented with orange and cinnamon, or fold into couscous along with roasted almonds and freshly chopped coriander (cilantro) leaves or parsley and serve alongside grilled (broiled) meats, or stuff a few prunes into your next roast chicken. Stew prunes in a little water or apple juice and serve with low-fat yoghurt for breakfast or as part of a fruit salad. Make a home-made trail mix using a combination of prunes, almonds, pepitas (pumpkin seeds) and sunflower seeds.

PUMPKIN (WINTER SQUASH) — This is one of my favourite vegetables, especially the Jap (Kent) variety. Pumpkin can be used in just about anything sweet or savoury — I like my pumpkin mashed with a little low-fat coconut milk and coriander (cilantro), used as a topping for beef and vegetable pies or oven-roasted with a little honey and cinnamon. Combine with wholemeal (whole-wheat) self-raising flour and sticky dates for yummy scones and cakes. Pumpkin is a good source of vitamins A and C, fibre, potassium and iron.

SEAWEED — When talking vegetables, we mustn't forget the importance of sea vegetables, especially seaweed. There are numerous varieties of seaweed and all are rich in essential minerals, and medical studies suggest they are effective in helping to prevent a variety of cancers. Here are the most common varieties:

- **Acrame** has a mild sea flavour, so it's a good choice when introducing sea vegetables into the diet. It needs to be soaked in water for about 5 minutes before using it. Add to steamed vegetables, salads or omelettes.
- **Agar agar** is a flavourless vegetarian gelling agent made from seaweed. It is high in protein and rich in minerals, and is used mainly to set desserts and puddings. It differs from gelatine in that it doesn't need chilling, but will set at room temperature in about 1 hour; substitute equal amounts of powdered agar agar for gelatine in recipes. It is also available as flakes, strands or blocks; use 1 teaspoon powdered agar agar for 1 tablespoon agar flakes.
- **Dulse** has a soft, chewy texture and a reddish-brown colour. It has a lovely mild taste and makes a great addition to salads. It doesn't need to be soaked before using.
- **Kelp** is available in flaked or powder form, so doesn't need soaking. Sprinkle a little over soups or add to dressings and salads.
- **Kombu** is a flat, wide green seaweed that is sold dried. It takes a while to soften, which is why it is perfect to add to nourishing vegetable and bean soups, or to casseroles made with lean meat, shiitakes and a little miso.
- **Nori** is used to make sushi, but it can also be added to soups, steamed rice or vegetables. You don't have to soak it, just use the sheets straight from the pack and cut with scissors into strips.
- **Wakame** needs to be soaked for 5 minutes before use. It can be added to salads, soups, omelettes, wraps and sandwiches. It is the traditional seaweed used in miso soup and has a lovely mild flavour of the sea.

SILVERBEET (SWISS CHARD) — High in folate, betacarotene and fibre, silverbeet can be used in the same way as English spinach. Make sure to trim the stalks and wash the leaves well. Use in stir-fries with garlic and ginger, steam with lemon juice and olive oil, purée with roasted garlic and basil or add to pies with ricotta, nutmeg and pepper.

SNOW PEAS (MANGETOUT) AND SUGAR SNAP PEAS — When I think of snow peas I immediately think of quick and easy stir-fries with oyster sauce, or a crisp salad with soy sauce and sesame seeds. Both of these greens are delicious served raw with dips, or lightly steamed and added to Asian-style salads. If adding to soups or stews toss them in just before serving, as they take only minutes to cook. Both snow peas and sugar snap peas are great sources of dietary fibre, protein, iron and the B vitamins.

SPROUTS (ALFALFA, BEAN, MUNG BEAN AND SNOW PEA) — All sprouts are a powerhouse of energy. Sprouted seeds are easily digested by the body and are a good source of fibre and vitamin C. Use mainly in salads, sandwiches and stir-fries. They make a great low-fat snack in between meals, so always keep a tub in the refrigerator.

STONE FRUITS (APRICOTS, NECTARINES, PEACHES AND PLUMS) — Their golden colours are an instant indication that stone fruits are rich in betacarotene and vitamin C. They are also a great source of minerals and fibre. Try to buy stone fruit that is ready for immediate use. Bake whole plums, nectarines, apricots and peaches in a little wine, sugar and spice and serve warm or at room temperature with low-fat vanilla yoghurt. Toss salad leaves with sliced ripe peaches and nectarines. Top with creamy low-fat ricotta and sprinkle with toasted walnuts. Make a stone fruit compote for breakfast by gently poaching the fruits in apple juice and a little spice.

SWEDES (RUTABAGA) AND TURNIPS — These root vegetables are best when cooked in soups or stews, or oven-roasted with garlic, lemon zest and fresh rosemary. They are also delicious when steamed and mashed with garlic, olive oil and chopped fresh parsley. They are good sources of vitamin C and fibre.

SWEET POTATO — This is a good source of vitamin A, C and E, folic acid, potassium, fibre, calcium, iron and phosphorus. It can be steamed, mashed or roasted. Fold in seasonal chopped vegetables to make instant vegetable fritters. Fold into low-fat scone and muffin mixes in place of butter. Make a warm sweet potato salad with fresh herbs, roasted almonds and a dressing of mandarin juice, honey and cinnamon.

TOMATO — There is nothing better than munching on a juicy, sun-ripened tomato on a hot day. Tomatoes are rich in lycopene, an antioxidant that helps prevent heart disease and cancer. They are also a good source of betacarotene and vitamins C and E. Highly versatile, they can be eaten like an apple or chopped up with basil, garlic and a little olive oil. Make a cool gazpacho or warming roasted tomato soup. Grill (broil) for breakfast and sprinkle with freshly ground black pepper, then serve with scrambled eggs and sautéed mushrooms.

WATERCRESS — Rich in antioxidants and minerals, watercress can be served with just about anything. Toss into salads with lean grilled (broiled) chicken breast and cucumber ribbons, or blend into a soup with English spinach and vegetable stock. Add to sandwiches made with sourdough rye bread, hard-boiled eggs and smoked salmon.

WITLOF (CHICORY/BELGIAN ENDIVE) — These wonderful leaves make a lovely salad or sensational stir-fry tossed with aromatics. Separate the leaves and use as a pocket for fillings such as tuna, bean dips, smoked salmon and pink grapefruit segments. I often make a salad of witlof leaves, walnuts, crisp pear, freshly ground black pepper, lemon or grapefruit juice and a little olive or linseed oil. They're a good source of vitamin C, folic acid and fibre.

ZUCCHINI (COURGETTES) — A good source of vitamin C, zucchini are also a great low-carbohydrate substitute for pasta and are the perfect diet food. Grate into thin spaghetti-like strands on a mandolin and use as you would pasta, for example with a freshly made tomato sauce flavoured with basil and roasted garlic. They can also be sliced lengthways and used in place of lasagne sheets. Mix raw grated zucchini with grated tofu, avocado and soy sauce and use in sushi rolls in place of rice.

Other superfoods

OILY FISH — Oily fish such as salmon, tuna, trout, sardines and mackerel provide the body with essential omega 3 fatty acids. These are polyunsaturated fats that cannot be manufactured by the body, so we need to get small amounts via our diet. Studies have discovered that omega 3 essential fatty acids help prevent cardiovascular disease, high cholesterol levels and heart attack, and are also vital for the healthy development of the eyes and brain, which is why pregnant women need to make sure they get enough of these fats in their diet. Current recommendations suggest that we should aim to have three fish meals a week.

Fish also provide iron and minerals, especially magnesium and potassium, which help regulate blood pressure. They are also a good source of B vitamins, particularly B12, which is important for a healthy nervous system.

GREEN TEA — This tea is rich in antioxidants. Studies show that those who consume one or two cups of green tea each day have a lower risk of certain cancers. Green tea has also been shown to increase the body's ability to burn body fat. Try replacing your regular tea or coffee with green tea.

OATS AND BARLEY — Two of the best complex carbohydrates, oats and barley are rich in soluble fibre and provide lasting energy. Soak overnight to make a yummy Bircher muesli or cook with water for a creamy porridge that will keep you full and satisfied all morning. You can even use oats and barley in place of white flour in apple crumble or use oat bran as a breadcrumb substitute for meat dishes and strudels.

WATER — Water is vital for life. Forget expensive face creams; pure water is an excellent anti-ageing tonic, as it helps to keep the skin hydrated, supple and fresh. We lose about 2.5 litres (87 fl oz) of water each day just through our everyday activities, so it's important to replace this lost fluid, and more if you're exercising most days, especially for those who sweat excessively. Make sure to replace lost body fluid with electrolytes, such as a gastrolyte sachet mixed with water. Be aware of sugar-laden sports drinks. Water also controls the appetite and keeps hunger pangs at bay. If you don't like the taste of water, you can make it a bit more appetizing by squeezing fresh lemon or lime juice into it; or make a large plunger of herbal tea using fresh or dried leaves, then drink it warm or cool.

Stocking the kitchen

When compiling your shopping list, keep in mind the following to help you make a healthy selection.

- Carbohydrates: Fresh vegetables, fruit and salads should make up at least 50 per cent of your daily intake. Choose from artichokes, avocados, dark green leafy vegetables, broccoli, cabbage, English spinach, lettuce, cherries, berries, apples, pears, oranges, pink grapefruit, melons, papaya, pineapple, apricots, beans, bean sprouts, eggplant (aubergine), capsicum (peppers), bok choy (pak choy), cucumbers, red kidney beans, adzuki beans, chickpeas, cannellini beans, lentils, carrots, sweet corn, cauliflower, brussels sprouts, mushrooms, tomatoes, turnips, pomegranates and snow peas (mangetout).

- **Protein**. At least 2–3 serves of protein are needed every day. Choose from fish such as salmon, mackerel, taylor, trevally, sardines and tuna; lean poultry like chicken or turkey without the skin; egg whites, low-fat cottage cheese, yoghurt, low-fat milk, soy milk, goat's milk and yoghurt, whey or soy protein powder, lean red meat, lentils, chickpeas, beans, tofu, tempeh, soya or adzuki beans, nuts and seeds.

- **Fats:** A small amount each day is all you need. Use extra virgin olive oil or linseed oil, whole or ground linseeds (flax seeds), nuts (such as almonds, cashews, hazelnuts, walnuts and macadamia nuts), pepitas (pumpkin seeds), sesame seeds and sunflower seeds, avocado or tahini. Keep refrigerated.

- **Grains:** Rolled (porridge) oats, oat bran, wheat germ, buckwheat, quinoa, millet, barley, brown and basmati rice, rye and dense wholegrain bread.

- **Beverages:** Water, green tea and herbal tea.

- **Condiments, spices and flavourings:** Mustard, soy sauce, mirin, balsamic vinegar, red wine vinegar, miso, black pepper, turmeric, dried herbs and spices, preservative-free and salt-reduced stock powder.

- **Sweeteners:** There is always room for a little sweetness in your life — just remember moderation. When making healthy cakes and desserts as part of your 20 per cent, once-a-week foods, I like to use less-refined, organic maple syrup, brown rice syrup, honey, molasses or apple juice concentrates. For low-kilojoule, low-carb and sugar-free sweeteners suitable for diabetics, use Xylitol or Splenda sweetener. Xylitol is a low-kilojoule alternative to sugar with about 40 per cent fewer kilojoules (calories). It is absorbed more slowly than sugar, therefore it doesn't contribute to a rapid rise in blood sugar that results in increased insulin in the body.

Reading food labels — what to look for

When buying foods, take a good look at the nutrition panel on the back of the packet and aim for these numbers where possible:

TOTAL FAT Aim for less than 10 g (1/4 oz) fat per 100 g (31/2 oz). Products that have 3 g (1/10 oz) or less per 100 g (31/2 oz) are categorized as low fat. Also choose products that are low in saturated fat.

LIQUIDS Look for less than 3 g (1/10 oz) fat per 100 ml (31/2 fl oz).

SUGAR Choose products with less than 25 g (1 oz) sugar per 100 g (31/2 oz).

SODIUM Choose low- or reduced-salt products.

FIBRE Three grams per serve is a good high-fibre choice. Aim for 30–40 g (1–11/2 oz) fibre per day.

Healthy cooking methods

We should all be practising healthy cooking methods if we want to stay lean for life. Here are some great ideas for how you can cook without adding extra fat and still retain the flavour and moisture in the food you love. Happy cooking!

BAKING AND ROASTING — The wonderful concentrated flavour and aroma of baked and roasted food are just too good to resist. So what's the difference between baked and roasted? Well, they actually mean the same thing, but are used for different recipes. Baking often refers to cakes and breads, while roasting often refers to meat and vegetables. Bake wholegrain breads, cakes and muffins using fruit and vegetable purées and low-fat yoghurt instead of butter. Use honey, juice concentrates or maple syrup instead of refined sugars, and wheat germ, dried fruits, nuts and seeds as toppings. When roasting, trim all visible fat from meat and cover the base of the tin with water or stock instead of oil. Add fresh herbs, then your chosen food. Roast vegetables in large chunks or keep whole. Sprinkle with a little stock, water or fruit juice to keep them moist during cooking.

BRAISING — This is my favourite way of cooking vegetables, tofu and lean meats. It essentially involves simmering ingredients in a flavoursome stock or sauce in a flameproof casserole dish or in the oven as a casserole-style hot pot. Think fish in spices with shiitake mushrooms, coq au vin, osso bucco, braised Savoy cabbage, braised silken tofu or broccoli in oyster sauce and you have the picture. The result is wonderfully delicious, tender and flavoursome meals without the use of added fat.

GRILLING (BROILING) AND BARBECUEING — Whether cooking food under or over direct high heat, it doesn't matter — the results are fantastic. You don't have to add any fat to the food, but if barbecuing, you may need to rub a little oil on the grill plate. Delicate fish can be wrapped in foil or banana leaves. Lean meat can be marinated in herbs, fruit juices and wine to add flavour (no need for oil marinades) and chunks of fruit can be brushed with honey and lime, then caramelized to perfection. You then need just a few accompaniments of salsas, mustards and yoghurt and you have a complete, easy meal.

POACHING — Poaching (and shallow poaching) is a delicious and quick way of cooking without any added fat, and better still, the poaching broth can be sipped with the meal or made into a flavoursome sauce. Poaching works best with fish or chicken, and when done correctly, the food is tender and moist. To poach, bring the poaching liquid to the boil, then reduce to a bare simmer. The liquid can be as simple as water, stock or juice. Fully immerse the food in the liquid, which must not be allowed to boil rapidly, as this can toughen the most delicate protein, and turn fruits into purées. Shallow poaching is a method normally applied to delicate seafood and chicken breast. The food is cooked in just a small amount of flavourful stock and aromatic ingredients until just tender. The remaining liquid is reduced and served with the dish as is, or thickened with a little arrowroot or cornflour (cornstarch) and then poured over the dish. If you want a creamy sauce, add a touch of evaporated skim milk to add richness but no fat. Poaching is a very quick process, so keep an eye on the simmering food. Fish takes 3–5 minutes depending on the thickness; chicken breasts take 8–12 minutes. Reduce the leftover cooking liquid by three-quarters to make a truly delicious light sauce.

SAUTÉING — Sautéing is another word for shallow-frying, but I do it without the excess fat. When cooking meats, make sure to heat the pan well over high heat before adding the meat. This will ensure you seal in the juices. A light spray of oil is all you need for the cooking. When sautéing without fat, it's also a good idea to add a little water or stock to the pan, a little at a time, to help with the cooking and retain the moisture in the food. Don't overdo it, however, or you'll have a bubbling stew instead.

STEAMING — This method of cooking is great for healthy eating, as the food is prepared with very little fat or oil. Nutrients are also retained because the food does not come into direct contact with the cooking liquid. Foods suited to steaming are vegetables, seafood, tofu, dumplings and tender chicken. Steamed foods may be finished off with a light squeeze of lemon, or you can add aromatics — such as offcuts from herbs and vegetables, spices such as star anise and cinnamon, or citrus peel — to the steaming water. For best results put 5 cm (2 inches) water or stock in a saucepan and bring to the boil. If you wish, add herbs or other aromatics to the water or stock. (The advantage of using stock is that the finished dish will be infused with the stock's flavours.) Put the food to be cooked into a steaming basket, put the basket into the saucepan and seal with a tight-fitting lid. Steam until the food is tender, 3–10 minutes depending on the type and thickness of the food. Asparagus and snow peas (mangetout) take only a few minutes; corn, broccoli, squash, cabbage, cauliflower and carrot take a little longer. If steaming a basket full of mixed vegetables, add the hardest and largest pieces first, then the most delicate.

Other ways of steaming are pan-steaming or cooking en papillote. Pan-steaming is usually used for vegetable dishes where the vegetables are cooked in a small amount of stock, juice or water, with aromatics added. The vegetables will cook and the liquid will reduce, creating a delicious flavoured sauce. It's very similar to braising and a good quick way to cook. Cooking en papillote involves baking food such as delicate seafood or vegetables in parchment (baking) paper or foil. Aromatics such as herbs or spices are added, and a little liquid such as stock, soy sauce, water or juice is drizzled over before sealing the parcel. The food is cooked by the steam created by the liquid.

STIR-FRYING — This is one of the fastest and healthiest ways to make a delicious meal. The idea behind stir-fry cooking is to cook food over high heat for a short amount of time with very little or no fat. Cooking quickly retains much of the valuable nutrients in the ingredients and allows vegetables to retain their crisp fresh quality. Stir-frying is usually done in a wok, but a good deep frying pan will also do nicely. The key to stir-frying is to cut the food into pieces of roughly the same size, so that the ingredients cook evenly and everything is ready at the same time. Hard vegetables such as carrots should be added to the wok before most of the other ingredients, and quick-cooking vegetables such as snow peas (mangetout) or bean sprouts should be thrown in just before serving. This prevents vegetables being either too hard or too limp. Your wok needs to be large enough to retain the high heat and allow you to keep the food moving rapidly. You can choose to stir-fry with or without oil; it's up to you. You can use a little peanut oil, water, wine or stock. Sesame oil is best added at the end of cooking, just before serving, to fully appreciate its flavour. In traditional Chinese and Asian cuisine, meat is used as a flavouring ingredient or as a supplement to the main dish — a little can go a long way if it is stir-fried with lots of crisp vegetables or noodles. The meat or seafood is usually cooked first until just done, then the vegetables and other flavourings are added. Marinating the meat first will also help it cook faster. Try marinating your meat in papaya or pineapple juice for tender, flavoursome meat.

Recipe make-overs

Let's face it — all of us crave our little comfort foods every now and again. It's not that we need the extra kilojoules (calories) or fat — it's just for the pure enjoyment of the food and the contentment we get from eating it. Here are some of my best make-over tips, so you can produce delicious heart-healthy versions of your favourite meals without the guilt. If you're on the 80/20 diet, make sure you keep the sweet treats as part of your 20 per cent once a week.

- When baking cakes and muffins, try replacing butter with unsaturated fats like light olive oil or macadamia nut oil. You can also reduce the amount of fat by replacing half or even three-quarters of the oil with a fruit purée such as apple, banana or prune. Apple purées are great because they have a neutral flavour and will blend with just about anything. Banana purées are better for carrot and banana cakes, and prune and date purées are perfect for chocolate cakes. The purée will add moisture to the cake or muffin. It also adds sweetness, so you can reduce the amount of sugar in the recipe. You usually don't notice the difference if you reduce the sugar by one-quarter or one-third in a cake or muffin recipe.
- Utilize flavourings like vanilla, citrus zest and sweet spices like cinnamon and nutmeg. Also, a light splash of a complementary liqueur goes a long way towards making a delicious low-fat make-over.
- Use wholemeal (whole-wheat) or spelt flour instead of refined white flour.
- When baking pies and tarts, use filo pastry in place of puff and shortcrust. As with baking cakes, when making your own pastry, substitute the butter with olive oil or a lovely, fragrant nut oil like macadamia.
- For a tasty, low-fat, gluten-free pastry base, ideal for savoury quiches and tarts, mix cooked rice with egg whites and press into the base of a lightly oiled pie dish. Bake in a moderate oven before filling and baking again to cook and set the filling.
- When using cream cheese in cheesecakes, use the low-fat varieties or choose low-fat blended cottage cheese or low-fat ricotta. Vegans can use silken tofu.
- Replace whole fat milk and yoghurt with low-fat varieties. If a recipe calls for whipped cream, use whipped low-fat ricotta combined with a little vanilla, honey and skim milk instead.
- Yoghurt can be used in place of sour cream in most cake and muffin recipes. You can also use cottage cheese blended with a little skim milk and a dash of lemon.
- When making creamy pastas, use low-fat milk thickened with a little cornflour (cornstarch) instead of cream. A light béchamel sauce made from skim milk similarly thickened can also be used in lasagne. You can even use skim milk blended with ricotta or cottage cheese. Vegetarians and vegans can make a lovely white sauce using blended silken tofu, or replace milk with soya milk.
- When cooking with meat, make sure you use nice lean cuts of meat or trim away any visible bits of fat before you cook with it. Remember also to remove the skin from poultry before eating.

- Get a non-stick frying pan and sauté in minimal oil or a little water or stock. Too many of us just add more oil if our food sticks to the pan. It's better to add small amounts of water throughout the cooking, which will keep the kilojoules down and maintain moisture in the food. The steam created also makes it quicker to cook. Remember, for every teaspoon of oil you cut, you save 180 kilojoules (43 calories)!

- When I make my hamburgers I always ask the butcher to mince up some lean topside steaks. Try it instead of the regular lean mince that you can buy in the supermarket — you'll definitely notice the difference in flavour and fat content. Serve with lots of yummy salad.

- Mince your own meat for bolognaise, rissoles, meatloaf and lasagne. Choose lean beef topside, veal, chicken or turkey breast.

- When cooking on the barbecue, forget the oil marinades and stick to citrus juices, wine, Asian marinades, herbs, spices, juices, papaya, pineapple and yoghurt to tenderize and flavour the meat.

- When using coconut milk for curries, use the low-fat versions or use evaporated skim milk and a little natural coconut extract.

- When making sandwiches, use healthy spreads in place of butter. Choose from avocado, tahini, hummus, mustards, pickles and low-fat mayonnaise.

- Mashed potatoes always seem to taste divine in a restaurant, but that's because of all the cream and butter that have been mixed through them. At home, just mash your spuds with a little skim milk and season to taste. Add flavour with freshly chopped herbs and oven-roasted garlic. When buying hot potato chips, remember that the chunkier the chip, the lower the fat. Better still, make your own chunky chips at home by oven-roasting with a little oil instead of using the deep-fryer.

- When making a risotto, omit the butter and cream and allow the natural flavours to come through from the stock and any fresh ingredients you add to the dish. Remember that rice marries well with just about any ingredient you may have on hand. Try folding through fresh seasonal baby vegetables, crabmeat, roasted onions and garlic, shellfish or ricotta.

- For a risotto with a difference, try folding purées of vegetable such as carrot, pumpkin (winter squash) or spinach into the finished rice before serving.

- If using hard cheeses in recipes, use low-fat varieties or smaller amounts of strongly flavoured cheeses like parmesan, where a little goes a long way.

- When a recipe asks for whole eggs, use 2 egg whites as a substitute for 1 egg. Egg whites are full of protein and contain no fat. Next time you make scrambled eggs for breakfast, use 1 whole egg and 5 egg whites. Cook in a non-stick pan with a light spray of vegetable oil, or in the microwave. Sprinkle over a little freshly ground black pepper and serve.

- Replace ready-made salad dressings with your own dressings made from citrus juices, vinegars and low-fat yoghurts mixed with fresh herbs or a little olive or linseed oil.

Eating out

When you're watching your weight, dining out can sometimes cause problems. Temptation often overrides willpower, preventing even the best of us from making sensible choices. It's still possible to follow the 80/20 diet and lose weight while eating out often, but you'll need to know a few do's and don'ts in order to stay on the straight and narrow.

- Try and have a look at the menu early so you can check out your choices. You can also enquire about the cooking methods if you are not sure and notify the chef if you have any specific dietary requirements. It is best to do this the day before, as it can sometimes be difficult for chefs to make changes to meals during peak-hour service.
- Don't starve yourself before going out to a restaurant. That way, you'll be much more in control when it comes to ordering and eating.
- Water, water, water is a must at the table. Drink lots of it.
- No alcohol! Or use it as part of your 20 per cent, once-a-week allowance.
- Keep the bread basket away from the table.
- When ordering soups, stick to consommés, clear vegetable broths or tomato-based soups. Creamy soups, chowders and veloutés contain a heap of fat in the form of cream, butter and egg yolks.
- Forget the fatty sauces when you dine out, or ask for them to be served on the side. Stay clear of hollandaise, béarnaise, béchamel, velouté, aïoli, or any cream or butter sauces. Opt for a squeeze of lemon juice or request a tomato-based sauce instead.
- When ordering vegetables, ask for them to be steamed or lightly stir-fried. Ask for vegetables and salads to come with the dressing on the side.
- If you want something sweet after dinner, ask for fresh fruit. If you just can't resist that chocolate cake on the menu, use it as part of your 20 per cent, once-a-week allocation and share it with someone else.

Buffets are often the worst places to eat too much. At breakfast buffets, be aware of greasy sausages and scrambled eggs cooked with lots of butter and cream. Other culprits to avoid are cheese omelettes, French toast and the waist-loving hollandaise on eggs benedict. It is also a good idea to check with the chef if that lovely dish of steaming porridge or velvety Bircher muesli is mixed with cream or full-fat milk. If it is, give it a miss and opt for healthier options like fresh fruit, low-fat yoghurt, miso soup and steamed rice. As well, no croissants, Danish or brioche, please — yes, they might taste good, but you'll soon be loosening up your belt or buying a larger pair of pants. For lunch and dinner, most buffets offer a wonderful array of delicious seafood, lean roast meats, leafy salads (without the dressing) and fresh fruit for dessert. Avoid the processed meat platter, pâté, anything in cheese sauce or creamy sauce, and anything deep-fried.

Cuisine choices

CHINESE — Choose steamed rice over fried rice, steamed dumplings rather than fried, and dishes with lots of vegetables, seafood, lean chicken or beef. Nothing fatty or deep-fried, such as spring rolls, fried duck and fatty pork. Omit rice and noodles from your evening meal.

FRENCH — Modern French cuisine is a lot healthier than it used to be, with much of it increasingly adopting a lighter Mediterranean style. Choose Provençal-style dishes based on vegetables, lean meat, chicken and seafood, rather than those rich in butter and cream sauces. Words like beurre blanc, meuniere, hollandaise and béarnaise are a no no — just ask for the sauce to be left off. Also give the duck confit a miss. This dish is essentially duck pieces fully immersed in saturated duck fat and simmered for 2–3 hours.

ITALIAN — Anything in a Neapolitan sauce is okay. For low-kilojoule options at night, avoid the pasta, lasagne, cannelloni and Bolognese dishes — basically anything with pasta — and instead choose leafy salads with the dressing on the side or steamed vegetables, and dishes such as osso bucco, saltimbocca and veal marsala (minus the butter). Grilled (broiled) or braised seafood dishes such as chilli mussels are also good choices. Steer clear of the garlic bread, polenta and risotto, as they are too high in both fat and carbohydrates.

JAPANESE — Most Japanese dishes are quite healthy. Just stay clear of tempura or anything in batter. Choose sushi, sashimi, seaweed salads and stir-fried, steamed or braised tofu, seafood, chicken and meat dishes. Japanese is a good choice when selecting take-away food for lunch or dinner. Forget anything with rice and noodles with your evening meal.

LEBANESE — Go for lean meat dishes, kebabs and fresh salads. Hummus and tabouleh are fine. Just stay clear of the warm, soft Lebanese bread that comes with the dips, and don't order the baklava.

MEXICAN — Forget corn chips, tacos and nachos loaded with cheese. Stick to burritos, fajitas, mole and chilli con carne cooked with lean beef, chicken or beans. Some Mexican places also offer grilled or barbecued seafood or chicken and salads. Forget any flat breads and rice with your evening meal and focus on light salads and vegetables.

THAI AND VIETNAMESE — Try all the delicious fragrant salads like green papaya or cabbage salad. Stick to steamed or poached fish and steamed vegetables, and ask for stir-fries to be cooked with a minimum of fat. Stay clear of anything deep-fried, the satay dishes, curries and soups containing coconut milk, and forgo the rice and noodle dishes at dinner.

Fast food

If you do have a hankering for fast food, try and keep it to no more than once a week. Keep it to the 20 per cent part of your diet. The good news is that most fast-food outlets now have a few healthier food options to choose from. For instance, choose roast chicken instead of fried chicken and eat it without the skin. Choose a thin-crust pizza with half the cheese and more vegetables and say no to the thick-crust meat-lover pizza or the extra cheesy pizzas. The healthy salad option is also a great idea! But don't forget to ask for the dressing on the side.

BURGERS — I prefer to make my own at home from lean organic meat and fresh salad, but if you must, choose a grilled chicken burger, minus the mayonnaise, cheese and bacon. Avoid the chips and instead have sides such as salad without the dressing.

CHICKEN — Choose chicken that has been barbecued rather than deep-fried and eat without the skin and stuffing. You can also include sides like a garden salad minus the dressing or a few cobs of corn and a small tub of peas.

DELI AND BAKERY FOOD — Choose fresh leafy salads and lean ham, turkey or tuna rolls without the mayonnaise or butter. Choose wholegrain bread instead of white and use healthy spreads like avocado, relish or mustard. If possible, request tuna that has been packed in brine or spring water not oil. Stay clear of meat pies, sausage rolls, any salads with mayonnaise, pasties, dim sum and the like.

FISH AND CHIPS — Choose grilled (broiled) fish and a side salad instead of deep-fried fish and chips — many fewer kilojoules (calories) and much less fat!

PIZZA — Choose two slices of a vegetarian thin and crispy pizza with half the cheese instead of the regular super supreme. In one easy step you will have halved the kilojoules and fat.

When on the road

Most people find it pretty difficult to find healthy choices when travelling by road. The trick is to be organized before the road trip. Pack the car with fresh fruit and bottled water. Tins of tuna, salmon and sardines make great quick snacks and so does low-fat yoghurt. If you find yourself hungry and have forgotten to prepare anything for your trip, most fast-food places have some healthy options on offer now and some good service stations have fresh fruit on hand; otherwise, look for low-fat yoghurt or a small pack of nuts.

Healthy kids

Childhood is the time when most eating patterns and food preferences are formed. Particularly around the ages of two to twelve years, children will come across many influences that may have a significant impact on their future as adults. When I was nine years old, my mother bought my lunch almost every day, as our school was right in town where she worked — I can also remember my lunch was always deep-fried chips or chicken or sausage, which I used to give away to the other children at school as I didn't want to eat such junk. She was horrified when I told her. This wasn't normal! But dear Mum finally relented after months of family arguments over why I refused to eat it and started giving me healthy sandwiches and fresh fruit instead.

I also remember being told that exercise wasn't ladylike, and it seemed like a constant battle with my parents to let me play sports. But with persistence, I got what I wanted in the end and I haven't stopped since. I believe you can do anything if you dream it and want it badly enough. Allowing yourself to become healthy and fit can happen at any age, even as young as nine. Parents need to educate themselves about food and exercise and take responsibility for their children's health. The television is not a baby-sitter and fast food is not nutritious food, it's just dead food. Obesity is an epidemic and we need to reverse the trend that is fast damaging our nation.

Fat cells are assembled in two growth periods during a child's life: early childhood and adolescence. Overeating during this period will increase the number of fat cells that are created in the body, so obese children can end up with two to three times more fat cells than an average child will have. Ultimately, the fat cells stop reproducing and this sets the fixed quota for the rest of their life. When a person gains or loses weight, it's the existing fat cells that simply swell or shrink to accommodate the change in fat levels. So, an overweight child is automatically capable of carrying more fat. All of this doesn't mean that such a child can't lose weight, it just means that they will have to work a lot harder through diet and exercise to see the results.

It's unfortunate that many kids today are both undernourished and fat. Undernourished because they are fed high-fat, high-sugar convenient meals like take-away pizzas, burgers, fried chicken, chips, hot dogs, pies, lollies, biscuits, chocolate and white bread, which contain little nutritional value but lots of fat, sugar and kilojoules. Many kids and families are living off this junk on a daily basis. These foods have also been linked with attention deficit disorder (ADD). Overweight children run a greater risk of becoming overweight adults and are more likely to develop health-related problems when they get older, such as heart disease, high blood pressure and diabetes. It is never too soon to encourage children to eat healthily and get them involved in outdoor sports and activities and away from the television and computer games. Remember, it's not about eating less food; it's about eating the right kinds of foods needed to build a strong, healthy body.

Food for healthy kids

A good breakfast is a must before heading off to school. Research suggests that if children miss the first meal of the day, their concentration deteriorates by late morning and they are unable to work as efficiently as those who ate a healthy breakfast. It's important to kick-start that metabolic rate and create energy for the rest of the day. For those children who have a hard time facing breakfast, fruit smoothies are a good choice. Just blend fruits like frozen berries and banana with milk and a little wheat germ and honey.

When it comes to lunch at the school canteen, choose wholegrain sandwiches and rolls filled with things like crisp salad, tuna, eggs and chicken. Fresh fruit always comes in handy and drinking lots of water is a must. Keep soft drinks and juices to a minimum. If children are bringing lunch from home, make sure lunchboxes are kept cool and stop bacteria breeding by placing a small iced drink or brick at the base.

Children often come home from school in the afternoon hungry. If they are in the habit of heading to the refrigerator for a binge, have lots of fruit for them to munch on. This is especially true for working mums and dads who finish late. Try to avoid takeaway and processed food. Instead, make sure to stock the refrigerator with lots of different varieties of fresh fruit, vegetable crudites, yoghurt, wholegrain breads and maybe some ready-prepared dishes that can be reheated in the microwave. Have on hand dinners like home-made soups or stews filled with lean meat and vegetables that are easy to reheat. Make your own healthy home-made burgers filled with lean meat and lots of fresh salad. Make your own low-fat oven chips rather than buying takeaway ones. Make your own pizzas and top with healthy toppings like fresh vegetables, chicken, turkey, salmon, tuna, spinach and fresh herbs. If your kids want something sweet after a meal, stick to fresh fruit salads, poached fruits or fruit crumbles. Make banana icy poles by placing bananas onto popsicle sticks, then into the freezer. Also encourage your children to eat at the table, not in front of the television or computer, and make sure they're drinking enough water, not soft drink full of sugar. Tired kids are often dehydrated kids.

Children need a variety of different healthy foods each day, including fruits, vegetables, wholegrains and lean protein. When talking healthy food, it is also very important to be careful of food choices for children under the age of 5 years. Small hard foods such as nuts, raw carrot and apple should be avoided, as they can easily block air passages. It is best to grate apples and carrots for young children and even cook them to soften a little. Make sure to remove all bones from foods such as chicken or fish, and encourage kids to sit quietly to eat and chew their food properly. Think about what you give to your kids and its effect on their nutrition. There are no excuses!

The other half of the health equation is regular exercise. It should be part of children's daily routine. Encourage and support them in their favourite activities. Joining various sporting clubs will not only keep them fit and active, but will also help their social skills, as they meet new friends with similar interests. Be a good role model for your children and be active yourself, and encourage your kids to participate in a variety of sports, not just one. Variety in sports will help them to develop a range of skills and develop their co-ordination and strength. If you're concerned about your child's weight, make sure you consult a dietician and your local doctor before starting any program.

What can you do about childhood obesity?

- Make sure your child eats a balanced diet with lots of assorted fruits and vegetables.
- Limit their intake of sugary drinks and encourage them to drink water.
- Plan meals and healthy snacks in advance.
- Eat home-cooked meals as a family, eating slowly and chewing the food well.
- Discourage eating meals and snacks when watching television.
- Encourage children to be involved in regular exercise, balancing the time spent in front of the TV or computer.
- Get the whole family involved in a healthy lifestyle.
- Have fun!

MENU PLANS AND RECIPES

Using the menu plans and recipes

In this section, you'll find more than 120 healthy recipes, which form the basis of my 12-week eating plan. The menu plan is made up of breakfast, lunch and dinner for each day, and vegetarian substitutions are given for many of the recipes that contain meat. I've also included some healthy snacks (see below), just in case you feel a little hungry in between meals. If you want a little more freedom with your diet, just use the menu plan as a guide and choose recipes from the book that you like. I have also provided recipes for healthy desserts and cakes that you can include as part of your 20 per cent, if you like.

Most breakfast and lunch recipes are designed for one person, while dinner is normally two to four serves, so adjust the portions accordingly. Aim to have at least eight glasses (2 litres/70 fl oz) water a day, complete around five hours of exercise per week (60 minutes a day) and get at least seven to eight hours of good-quality sleep each night.

One helpful tool is a food and exercise diary. I would like you to start writing down everything you eat and drink each day. The diary will help keep you honest and on track. At the top of each day's entry, write down and read through the affirmations on the following pages. These will also help you stay positive and motivated throughout the 12 weeks, and develop good habits for the long term. Each time you eat, just take a moment to think about what you are putting into your mouth. Ask yourself, is this good for me?

In your diary, also keep a record of the following:

AQUA METER (glasses): 1 2 3 4 5 6 7 8 9 10

WORKOUT INTENSITY: Heavy/Medium/Light

HOURS OF SLEEP: _____

ENERGY LEVELS: Great/Average/Poor

HEALTHY SNACKS

1 Whole seasonal fresh fruit
2 A bowl of fresh green soya beans
3 A small handful of raw nuts (almonds, cashews) and seeds
4 A tub of diet yoghurt
5 Sugar-free protein shake made with water
6 A small tin of seafood in spring water
7 Hard-boiled egg whites
8 Raw vegetables with hummus or skim-milk cottage cheese
9 Low-fat latte or hot chocolate
10 Diet jelly

Eat three healthy meals a day

BREAKFAST — This is the meal that breaks the fast your body has endured since the previous evening's meal, which may have been as much as 14 hours ago, depending on when you last ate and what time you got up. Studies have shown that people who don't eat breakfast tend to overeat at lunch and dinner, and so gain weight. Aim to eat a balanced, healthy breakfast with a relatively low glycaemic index (GI). Low-GI foods are those that release their energy at a slower, more even rate. Try to include some protein and low-GI carbohydrates. Eating low-GI foods will kick-start a sluggish metabolic rate, keep blood sugars stable and energize you for the rest of your day. By making breakfast and lunch your main meals, instead of dinner, you will have better success in controlling your metabolism and staying lean throughout life. As well, restrict coffee to about 2 cups per day. Too much caffeine can lead to dehydration, sluggishness, insomnia, anxiety and depression, as well as affect the body's ability to absorb iron. You could also replace your coffee with green tea.

Now, I've given you plenty of breakfast ideas to choose from and they all take around 5 minutes to whip up, so there are no excuses! Even the busiest person should be able to manage it.

LUNCH — Even if you've had a good breakfast, it's important that you also have a good healthy lunch. Your body is still active, so the food you eat will be burned off more readily and will help you make it through the rest of the afternoon. People who skip lunch often end up craving fats and sugar by mid-afternoon, so they start eating unhealthy snacks and also tend to overeat when it comes to dinner.

Planning is essential for a healthy lunch, especially if you work in an area that sells only greasy fast food, leaving you no healthy options. It should be a combination of lean protein, wholegrains, fruits and vegetables. It is a good idea to plan lunches a week at a time, to make shopping easier, and to do the prep work the night before, rather than when you're half-asleep in the morning. Make salads without dressing (add the dressing just before eating, or the salad will go limp and soggy). Make the most of workplace refrigerators and microwaves, too. If you have to go out for lunch, choose the healthiest options possible. Stay clear of coleslaw, potato salad and pasta salad, as they're full of fat. Order lean protein and leafy salads in restaurants, and ask for sauces and dressings to be on the side.

Feeling tired and fatigued in the afternoon is often a sign that your body is dehydrated. Toxins build up in your blood stream making you feel tired and sluggish. It's especially common in winter when we tend to drink more coffee to warm up, not realizing that we are dehydrating our body at the same time. Have a 1-litre (35 fl oz) water bottle with you at your desk and make sure you drink up! It will keep you alert and help your body eliminate toxins. If you're not too keen on all that water, try it with a squeeze of lemon, or just sip on refreshing herbal teas such as peppermint and lemon grass.

DINNER — This is the time of day where our body starts to slow down for the night. If you're not running marathons, dinner should focus on a healthy mix of water-based, high-fibre vegetables and lean protein. Remember, no high-kilojoule complex carbohydrates such as bread, pasta, rice, noodles, potato, refined white sugar and alcohol. If you're still hungry after your meal, there is nothing better than sweet, juicy fresh fruit.

The ideal day

Wake up: Drink 2 glasses of water

Workout: 60 minutes

Shower and get ready.

BREAKFAST

Choose from fresh seasonal fruit and vegetables, low-GI wholegrains such as wholemeal (whole-wheat) or rye bread, oats, barley, quinoa, millet, buckwheat and basmati rice; low-fat dairy, such as cottage cheese or yoghurt; organic eggs, seafood, beans, tofu, protein shake, raw nuts and seeds. Also, 2 cups green tea.

MORNING SNACK (optional)

Choose one item from the list on page 52.

LUNCH

Choose from leafy green salads or vegetables with added lean protein such as chicken breast, egg white, cottage cheese, beans, seafood, tofu or lean meat. Add your own salad dressing made from the recipes listed or use a light squeeze of lemon juice or drizzle of balsamic and 1 tablespoon flax seed (linseed) or olive oil. You can also make a warming pot of vegetable soup in cooler months in place of the salads. Just make sure to add a little lean protein.

AFTERNOON SNACK (optional)

Choose one item from the list on page 52.

DINNER

Choose lean protein such as chicken without the skin, fish, red meat, tofu or egg whites. Eat lower carb vegetables and salads with dinner. Avoid rice, pasta, bread, potato, turnip and swede (rutabaga) at dinner time only.

Tips:
- Drink 8 glasses (2 litres/70 fl oz) of water every day
- Try to exercise 5 days a week for up to 60 minutes
- Always eat a good breakfast
- Don't overeat at dinner
- Avoid or eat less white bread and crisp breads, refined sugar, alcohol, processed meats, biscuits, cakes, lollies, pastry, soft drinks.

The ten rules of the 80/20 diet

1. SHOP WISELY — Plan your menus for the week, including healthy snacks. This way you'll avoid impulse buying and takeaway foods. Don't go shopping if you're hungry and always have a shopping list.

2. COOK SIMPLE AND LIGHT — The best healthy cooking methods are steaming, poaching, baking and roasting, grilling (broiling) and stir-frying. Avoid saturated fat in recipes and in cooking. Sauté meat and vegetables in a non-stick pan with 1 teaspoon oil, then add a little stock or water during cooking to stop sticking and retain moisture.

3. EAT THE RIGHT WAY — Eat in moderation. Eat lots of fruit, vegetables, lean protein, wholegrains, raw nuts and seeds about 80 per cent of the time. About 20 per cent of the time you can indulge your cravings — in moderation. As well, eat slowly; this will help digestion and regulate the amount you eat. If you eat out often, read the menu carefully before ordering. Avoid deep-fried food and order dressings and sauces on the side. For dessert, order fresh fruits and sorbets, or share an indulgence with a friend as part of your 20 per cent.

4. DRINK PLENTY OF WATER — Water is vital for life, is an excellent anti-ageing tonic, controls the appetite and keeps hunger pangs at bay. Aim to drink about 8 glasses (2 litres/70 fl oz) water a day. Before, during and after exercising, it is important to increase water consumption to prevent dehydration, especially in hot weather.

5. ENJOY YOUR EXERCISE — Fun is the key word here. You have to enjoy your exercise, especially if it's going to be part of your everyday lifestyle. Vary it to make it interesting; that way, you won't get bored with your workouts. Challenge yourself and set goals. If you need motivation and encouragement, exercise with a friend.

6. DO STRENGTH TRAINING — Weight training is important in increasing metabolic rate. It keeps you lean and toned and is one of the best ways to encourage your body to utilize more fat as fuel. Also, 1 kg (2 lb 4 oz) of muscle burns 400 kilojoules (100 calories) per day; the same amount of fat burns only 16 kilojoules (4 calories).

7. KEEP MOVING AND SET REALISTIC GOALS — Don't set goals that you know are unattainable for your natural body composition. Make time to exercise at least 5 days a week. It doesn't matter what you do, so long as you just move.

8. WORK ON YOUR FLEXIBILITY — Flexibility training (stretching) helps decrease muscle soreness and increases mobility, reducing the rate of injury.

9. STAY POSITIVE AND PUT YOURSELF FIRST — To enjoy everyday life, we need to put ourselves first and look after ourselves. The best things you can do for your body are to nourish yourself with healthy foods and get regular exercise and plenty of rest. A positive approach is the best way to tackle anything.

10. MAKE TIME FOR RELAXATION — Sleep and relaxation are essential for the body and mind to revive, repair and recharge. Learning to relax can also help reduce stress and anxiety.

Week one: suggested menu plan

	BREAKFAST	LUNCH	DINNER	SNACKS (OPTIONAL)
MONDAY	natural vanilla muesli with pistachio, fig, orange and apricot	Greek salad with tuna and balsamic dressing	spicy braised fish with shiitake mushrooms	choose 1–2 from the list on page 52
TUESDAY	fried egg whites with cheese and tomato	chicken and vegetable soup	spicy laksa	choose 1–2 from the list on page 52
WEDNESDAY	natural vanilla muesli with pistachio, fig, orange and apricot	Greek salad with tuna and balsamic dressing	Thai prawn salad	choose 1–2 from the list on page 52
THURSDAY	fried egg whites with cheese and tomato	chicken and vegetable soup	stir-fried chicken and snowpeas	choose 1–2 from the list on page 52
FRIDAY	natural vanilla muesli with pistachio, fig, orange and apricot	Greek salad with tuna and balsamic dressing	vegetable curry	choose 1–2 from the list on page 52
SATURDAY	YOUR CHOICE	YOUR CHOICE	YOUR CHOICE	YOUR CHOICE
SUNDAY	fried egg whites with cheese and tomato	smoked salmon and lettuce wraps	chicken meatloaf	choose 1–2 from the list on page 52

Affirmation for week one

Whatever you believe you can achieve

Week two: suggested menu plan

	BREAKFAST	LUNCH	DINNER	SNACKS (OPTIONAL)
MONDAY	creamy scrambled eggs on toast	chicken and prawn salad with avocado, mango and chilli sauce	my best smoked salmon caesar salad	choose 1–2 from the list on page 52
TUESDAY	summer berries with almonds	chilli bean and guacamole lettuce wraps	oven-baked fish fillet	choose 1–2 from the list on page 52
WEDNESDAY	creamy scrambled eggs on toast	chicken and prawn salad with avocado, mango and chilli sauce	chilli mussels	choose 1–2 from the list on page 52
THURSDAY	summer berries with almonds	chilli bean and guacamole lettuce wraps	mushroom soup with fish, lime and coriander	choose 1–2 from the list on page 52
FRIDAY	creamy scrambled eggs on toast	chicken and prawn salad with avocado, mango and chilli sauce	pork and vegetable san choi bao	choose 1–2 from the list on page 52
SATURDAY	YOUR CHOICE	YOUR CHOICE	YOUR CHOICE	YOUR CHOICE
SUNDAY	summer berries with almonds	spinach and ricotta mushroom pizzas	lean chilli con carne	choose 1–2 from the list on page 52

Affirmation for week two

Yes I can!

Week three: suggested menu plan

	BREAKFAST	LUNCH	DINNER	SNACKS (OPTIONAL)
MONDAY	strawberry power smoothie	chicken salad with honey mustard dressing	veal saltimbocca with rocket and parmesan salad	choose 1–2 from the list on page 52
TUESDAY	sardines with tomato and spinach on toast	smoked salmon and lettuce wraps	mushroom soup with fish, lime and coriander	choose 1–2 from the list on page 52
WEDNESDAY	strawberry power smoothie	chicken salad with honey mustard dressing	Egyptian lamb salad	choose 1–2 from the list on page 52
THURSDAY	sardines with tomato and spinach on toast	smoked salmon and lettuce wraps	veal cutlets with sautéed spinach	choose 1–2 from the list on page 52
FRIDAY	strawberry power smoothie	chicken salad with honey mustard dressing	turbo red chicken curry	choose 1–2 from the list on page 52
SATURDAY	YOUR CHOICE	YOUR CHOICE	YOUR CHOICE	YOUR CHOICE
SUNDAY	sardines with tomato and spinach on toast	steamed white fish with mango relish	roast chicken salad with hazelnut dressing	choose 1–2 from the list on page 52

Affirmation for week three

Live the life you've imagined

Week four: suggested menu plan

	BREAKFAST	LUNCH	DINNER	SNACKS (OPTIONAL)
MONDAY	papaya stuffed with berries and passionfruit	chunky vegetable soup	warm beef salad	choose 1–2 from the list on page 52
TUESDAY	linseed porridge	chicken and pinepple coleslaw	turbo red chicken curry	choose 1–2 from the list on page 52
WEDNESDAY	papaya stuffed with berries and passionfruit	chunky vegetable soup	crab omelette	choose 1–2 from the list on page 52
THURSDAY	linseed porridge	chicken and pinepple coleslaw	stir-fried garlic and chilli king prawns	choose 1–2 from the list on page 52
FRIDAY	papaya stuffed with berries and passionfruit	chunky vegetable soup	vegetable tagine	choose 1–2 from the list on page 52
SATURDAY	YOUR CHOICE	YOUR CHOICE	YOUR CHOICE	YOUR CHOICE
SUNDAY	linseed porridge	Thai fish cakes with cucumber, lime and chilli sauce	the lean shepherd's pie	choose 1–2 from the list on page 52

Affirmation for week four

I love to exercise

Week five: suggested menu plan

	BREAKFAST	LUNCH	DINNER	SNACKS (OPTIONAL)
MONDAY	natural vanilla muesli with pistachio, fig, orange and apricot	Greek salad with tuna and balsamic dressing	spicy braised fish with shiitake mushrooms	choose 1–2 from the list on page 52
TUESDAY	fried egg whites with cheese and tomato	chicken and vegetable soup	spicy laksa	choose 1–2 from the list on page 52
WEDNESDAY	natural vanilla muesli with pistachio, fig, orange and apricot	Greek salad with tuna and balsamic dressing	Thai prawn salad	choose 1–2 from the list on page 52
THURSDAY	fried egg whites with cheese and tomato	chicken and vegetable soup	stir-fried chicken and snowpeas	choose 1–2 from the list on page 52
FRIDAY	natural vanilla muesli with pistachio, fig, orange and apricot	Greek salad with tuna and balsamic dressing	vegetable curry	choose 1–2 from the list on page 52
SATURDAY	YOUR CHOICE	YOUR CHOICE	YOUR CHOICE	YOUR CHOICE
SUNDAY	fried egg whites with cheese and tomato	smoked salmon and lettuce wraps	chicken meatloaf	choose 1–2 from the list on page 52

Affirmation for week five

There are no excuses

Week six: suggested menu plan

	BREAKFAST	LUNCH	DINNER	SNACKS (OPTIONAL)
MONDAY	creamy scrambled eggs on toast	chicken and prawn salad with avocado, mango and chilli sauce	my best smoked salmon caesar salad	choose 1–2 from the list on page 52
TUESDAY	summer berries with almonds	chilli bean and guacamole lettuce wraps	oven-baked fish fillet	choose 1–2 from the list on page 52
WEDNESDAY	creamy scrambled eggs on toast	chicken and prawn salad with avocado, mango and chilli sauce	chilli mussels	choose 1–2 from the list on page 52
THURSDAY	summer berries with almonds	chilli bean and guacamole lettuce wraps	mushroom soup with fish, lime and coriander	choose 1–2 from the list on page 52
FRIDAY	creamy scrambled eggs on toast	chicken and prawn salad with avocado, mango and chilli sauce	pork and vegetable san choi bao	choose 1–2 from the list on page 52
SATURDAY	YOUR CHOICE	YOUR CHOICE	YOUR CHOICE	YOUR CHOICE
SUNDAY	summer berries with almonds	spinach and ricotta mushroom pizzas	lean chilli con carne	choose 1–2 from the list on page 52

Affirmation for week six

I am responsible for my own actions

Week seven: suggested menu plan

	BREAKFAST	LUNCH	DINNER	SNACKS (OPTIONAL)
MONDAY	red papaya and strawberry smoothie	chicken salad with honey mustard dressing	veal saltimbocca with rocket and parmesan salad	choose 1–2 from the list on page 52
TUESDAY	sardines with tomato and spinach on toast	smoked salmon and lettuce wraps	mushroom soup with fish, lime and coriander	choose 1–2 from the list on page 52
WEDNESDAY	red papaya and strawberry smoothie	chicken salad with honey mustard dressing	Egyptian lamb salad	choose 1–2 from the list on page 52
THURSDAY	sardines with tomato and spinach on toast	smoked salmon and lettuce wraps	veal cutlets with sautéed spinach	choose 1–2 from the list on page 52
FRIDAY	red papaya and strawberry smoothie	chicken salad with honey mustard dressing	turbo red chicken curry	choose 1–2 from the list on page 52
SATURDAY	YOUR CHOICE	YOUR CHOICE	YOUR CHOICE	YOUR CHOICE
SUNDAY	sardines with tomato and spinach on toast	steamed white fish with mango relish	roast chicken salad with hazelnut dressing	choose 1–2 from the list on page 52

Affirmation for week seven

I am strong, fit and beautiful

Week eight: suggested menu plan

	BREAKFAST	LUNCH	DINNER	SNACKS (OPTIONAL)
MONDAY	papaya stuffed with berries and passionfruit	chunky vegetable soup	warm beef salad	choose 1–2 from the list on page 52
TUESDAY	linseed porridge	chicken and pineapple coleslaw	turbo red chicken curry	choose 1–2 from the list on page 52
WEDNESDAY	papaya stuffed with berries and passionfruit	chunky vegetable soup	crab omelette	choose 1–2 from the list on page 52
THURSDAY	linseed porridge	chicken and pineapple coleslaw	stir-fried garlic and chilli king prawns	choose 1–2 from the list on page 52
FRIDAY	papaya stuffed with berries and passionfruit	chunky vegetable soup	vegetable tagine	choose 1–2 from the list on page 52
SATURDAY	YOUR CHOICE	YOUR CHOICE	YOUR CHOICE	YOUR CHOICE
SUNDAY	linseed porridge	Thai fish cakes with cucumber, lime and sweet chilli sauce	the lean shepherd's pie	choose 1–2 from the list on page 52

Affirmation for week eight

I can do anything

Week nine: suggested menu plan

	BREAKFAST	LUNCH	DINNER	SNACKS (OPTIONAL)
MONDAY	natural vanilla muesli with pistachio, fig, orange and apricot	Greek salad with tuna and balsamic dressing	spicy braised fish with shiitake mushrooms	choose 1–2 from the list on page 52
TUESDAY	fried egg whites with cheese and tomato	chicken and vegetable soup	spicy laksa	choose 1–2 from the list on page 52
WEDNESDAY	natural vanilla muesli with pistachio, fig, orange and apricot	Greek salad with tuna and balsamic dressing	Thai prawn salad	choose 1–2 from the list on page 52
THURSDAY	fried egg whites with cheese and tomato	chicken and vegetable soup	stir-fried chicken and snow peas	choose 1–2 from the list on page 52
FRIDAY	natural vanilla muesli with pistachio, fig, orange and apricot	Greek salad with tuna and balsamic dressing	vegetable curry	choose 1–2 from the list on page 52
SATURDAY	YOUR CHOICE	YOUR CHOICE	YOUR CHOICE	YOUR CHOICE
SUNDAY	fried egg whites with cheese and tomato	smoked salmon and lettuce wraps	chicken meatloaf	choose 1–2 from the list on page 52

Affirmation for week nine

I am in charge of my destiny

Week ten: suggested menu plan

	BREAKFAST	LUNCH	DINNER	SNACKS (OPTIONAL)
MONDAY	creamy scrambled eggs on toast	chicken and prawn salad with avocado, mango and chilli sauce	my best smoked salmon caesar salad	choose 1–2 from the list on page 52
TUESDAY	summer berries with almonds	chilli bean and guacamole lettuce wraps	oven-baked fish fillet	choose 1–2 from the list on page 52
WEDNESDAY	creamy scrambled eggs on toast	chicken and prawn salad with avocado, mango and chilli sauce	chilli mussels	choose 1–2 from the list on page 52
THURSDAY	summer berries with almonds	chilli bean and guacamole lettuce wraps	mushroom soup with fish, lime and coriander	choose 1–2 from the list on page 52
FRIDAY	creamy scrambled eggs on toast	chicken and prawn salad with avocado, mango and chilli sauce	pork and vegetable san choi bao	choose 1–2 from the list on page 52
SATURDAY	YOUR CHOICE	YOUR CHOICE	YOUR CHOICE	YOUR CHOICE
SUNDAY	summer berries with almonds	spinach and ricotta mushroom pizzas	lean chilli con carne	choose 1–2 from the list on page 52

Affirmation for week ten

Follow your dreams

Week eleven: suggested menu plan

	BREAKFAST	LUNCH	DINNER	SNACKS (OPTIONAL)
MONDAY	banana and blueberry smoothie	chicken salad with honey mustard dressing	veal saltimbocca with rocket and parmesan salad	choose 1–2 from the list on page 52
TUESDAY	sardines with tomato and spinach on toast	smoked salmon and lettuce wraps	mushroom soup with fish, lime and coriander	choose 1–2 from the list on page 52
WEDNESDAY	banana and blueberry smoothie	chicken salad with honey mustard dressing	Egyptian lamb salad	choose 1–2 from the list on page 52
THURSDAY	sardines with tomato and spinach on toast	smoked salmon and lettuce wraps	veal cutlets with sautéed spinach	choose 1–2 from the list on page 52
FRIDAY	banana and blueberry smoothie	chicken salad with honey mustard dressing	turbo red chicken curry	choose 1–2 from the list on page 52
SATURDAY	YOUR CHOICE	YOUR CHOICE	YOUR CHOICE	YOUR CHOICE
SUNDAY	sardines with tomato and spinach on toast	steamed white fish with mango relish	roast chicken salad with hazelnut dressing	choose 1–2 from the list on page 52

Affirmation for week eleven

I am healthy and happy

Week twelve: suggested menu plan

	BREAKFAST	LUNCH	DINNER	SNACKS (OPTIONAL)
MONDAY	papaya stuffed with berries and passionfruit	chunky vegetable soup	warm beef salad	choose 1–2 from the list on page 52
TUESDAY	linseed porridge	chicken and pineapple coleslaw	turbo red chicken curry	choose 1–2 from the list on page 52
WEDNESDAY	papaya stuffed with berries and passionfruit	chunky vegetable soup	crab omelette	choose 1–2 from the list on page 52
THURSDAY	linseed porridge	chicken and pineapple coleslaw	stir-fried garlic and chilli king prawns	choose 1–2 from the list on page 52
FRIDAY	papaya stuffed with berries and passionfruit	chunky vegetable soup	vegetable tagine	choose 1–2 from the list on page 52
SATURDAY	YOUR CHOICE	YOUR CHOICE	YOUR CHOICE	YOUR CHOICE
SUNDAY	linseed porridge	Thai fish cakes with cucumber, lime and sweet chilli sauce	the lean shepherd's pie	choose 1–2 from the list on page 52

Affirmation for week twelve

Perseverance is the only way to success

BREAKFAST

Natural vanilla muesli with pistachio, fig, orange and apricot

Makes 12 servings

400 g (14 oz/4 cups) rolled (porridge) oats
125 g (4½ oz/1 cup) rice bran
40 g (1½ oz/½ cup) wheat germ
15 g (½ oz/¼ cup) linseeds (flax seeds)
100 g (3½ oz) pistachio nuts, chopped
30 g (1 oz/¼ cup) sunflower seeds
40 g (1½ oz/¼ cup) pepitas (pumpkin seeds)
125 g (4½ oz) dried figs, sliced
125 g (4½ oz) dried apricots, chopped
1 teaspoon ground cinnamon
zest from 1 orange
1 vanilla bean, halved lengthways (optional)

Combine the rolled oats, rice bran, wheat germ, linseeds, pistachio nuts, sunflower seeds, pepitas, figs, apricots, cinnamon and orange zest. Add the vanilla bean, if using. Store in the refrigerator in an airtight container.

To serve, soak 70 g (2½ oz/½ cup) muesli in 125 ml (4 fl oz/½ cup) low-fat milk or apple juice overnight. Fold through 1 freshly grated apple or pear and 100 g (3½ oz/heaped ⅓ cup) low-fat plain yoghurt.

Note You can reuse the vanilla bean in your next batch of muesli, or wash and dry it and use it in another recipe. Each vanilla bean can be used thus several times.

Summer berries with almonds

Serves 1

250 g (9 oz) strawberries, washed and halved
70 g (2½ oz) blueberries
200 g (7 oz/heaped ¾ cup) low-fat plain yoghurt or vanilla soy cream (see Note)
6 almonds, chopped (about 1 tablespoon)

Combine the strawberries and blueberries. Layer into a glass or bowl with the yoghurt or soy cream. Top with the chopped almonds and serve.

Note To make the vanilla soy cream, combine in a food processor 300 g (10½ oz) silken tofu with 2 teaspoons honey or maple syrup and 2 teaspoons natural vanilla extract. Process until smooth and creamy. Drizzle half over the mixed berries and top with the almonds. Store the remaining soy cream in the refrigerator.

Honey-toasted muesli with almonds, sultanas, apple and apricot

Makes 12 servings

400 g (14 oz/4 cups) rolled (porridge) oats
100 g (3^1/$_2$ oz) almonds, chopped
90 g (3^1/$_4$ oz/^{1}/$_4$ cup) honey, warmed
125 g (4^1/$_2$ oz/1 cup) rice bran
40 g (1^1/$_2$ oz/^{1}/$_2$ cup) wheat germ
30 g (1 oz/^{1}/$_4$ cup) sunflower seeds
40 g (1^1/$_2$ oz/^{1}/$_4$ cup) pepitas (pumpkin seeds)
15 g (^{1}/$_2$ oz/^{1}/$_4$ cup) linseeds (flax seeds)
60 g (2^1/$_4$ oz) dried apples, chopped
125 g (4^1/$_2$ oz) dried apricots, chopped
125 g (4^1/$_2$ oz/1 cup) sultanas (golden raisins)
1 teaspoon ground cinnamon
zest from 1 orange

Preheat the oven to 200°C (400°F/Gas 6). Combine the rolled oats and almonds, then tip into a baking tin lined with foil or baking paper. Toast in the oven until golden, tossing occasionally to ensure an even colour.

Remove from the oven and pour into a large bowl. Stir through the honey and allow to cool completely until crisp. Add the rice bran, wheat germ, seeds, apple, apricot, sultanas, cinnamon and orange zest and stir together well.

Store in an airtight container in the refrigerator until needed. Serve with low-fat plain yoghurt and fresh fruit.

Linseed porridge

Serves 1

15 g (^{1}/$_2$ oz/^{1}/$_4$ cup) linseeds (flax seeds)
100 g (3^1/$_2$ oz/heaped ^{1}/$_3$ cup) low-fat plain yoghurt
1 apple, grated
pinch of ground cinnamon

Combine the linseeds and 125 ml (4 fl oz/^{1}/$_2$ cup) water and leave to soak overnight in the refrigerator.

Fold through the yoghurt, apple and cinnamon.

Note You can also stir through a little sweetener to taste.

Home-made gluten-free muesli

Makes 12 servings

120 g (4^1/$_4$ oz/4 cups) toasted rice flake cereal
100 g (3^1/$_2$ oz/4 cups) puffed amaranth (see Note)
250 g (9 oz/2 cups) rice bran
100 g (3^1/$_2$ oz/1 cup) flaked almonds, toasted
30 g (1 oz/^{1}/$_4$ cup) sunflower seeds
40 g (1^1/$_2$ oz/^{1}/$_4$ cup) pepitas (pumpkin seeds)
15 g (^{1}/$_2$ oz/^{1}/$_4$ cup) linseeds (flax seeds)
125 g (4^1/$_2$ oz/1 cup) sultanas (golden raisins)
150 g (5^1/$_2$ oz) dried pears, chopped

Combine the rice flakes, amaranth, rice bran, almonds, seeds, sultanas and pears in an airtight container. Store in the refrigerator until needed. Serve with low-fat milk and seasonal fruit.

Note Puffed amaranth can be found in the cereal aisle in most major supermarkets and in health food stores. It is gluten-free and high in protein, with a nutty taste. It can be eaten on its own, topped with skim milk and sliced banana, or used as a crumbing mix for foods such as fish cakes and veal schnitzel. Amaranth flour is also available; it's great for gluten-free cakes, muffins and pancakes.

Oat bran porridge with banana and blueberries

Serves 1

50 g (1^3/$_4$ oz/^{1}/$_3$ cup) oat bran
1 tablespoon linseeds (flax seeds)
1 tablespoon wheat germ
125 ml (4 fl oz/^{1}/$_2$ cup) low-fat milk or soya milk
1 banana, sliced
50 g (1^3/$_4$ oz/^{1}/$_3$ cup) blueberries
1 teaspoon honey, to serve (optional)

Combine the oat bran, linseeds, wheat germ, milk and 185 ml (6 fl oz/^{3}/$_4$ cup) water in a saucepan. Cook over medium heat for about 5 minutes, or until the porridge is thick and creamy. Spoon into a serving bowl and top with the sliced banana and blueberries. Drizzle over a little honey, if using, and serve.

Note The blueberries can be replaced with other fruit such as strawberries, raspberries or peaches.

Omelette with tomatoes, smoked salmon and rocket

Serves 1

1 egg
5 egg whites
6 cherry tomatoes, halved, or 1 tomato, chopped
50 g (1³/₄ oz) sliced smoked salmon
1 handful rocket (arugula)

Beat the egg, egg whites and some freshly ground black pepper in a small bowl. Pour into a hot non-stick oven-proof frying pan. Stir gently to get rid of any runny bits, then allow the base to firm slightly. Top with the tomato and place under a hot grill (broiler) to warm through.

Slide the omelette onto a serving plate. Top with the smoked salmon and rocket, then serve.

Note Tinned red salmon can be used in place of the smoked salmon, and vegetarians can omit the salmon altogether. Sprinkle with finely shredded basil, if you like.

Bruschetta with soft poached egg and tomato

Serves 1

1 roma (plum) tomato, peeled and chopped
1 tablespoon chopped basil
1 slice good-quality sourdough bread
1 garlic clove
1 egg

Combine the chopped tomato, basil and a little freshly ground black pepper in a bowl, then set aside. Toast the bread under the grill (broiler) on both sides, then rub with the garlic.

Boil a small saucepan of water and add a splash of vinegar or lemon juice. Reduce the heat, crack the egg into the pan and simmer for 3 minutes, or until the egg is softly poached. Remove the egg with a slotted spoon. Top the toast with the tomato mixture, then the egg.

Pineapple and papaya salad with yoghurt and crunchy bits

Serves 2

1 small red papaya, seeded and chopped
1 small pineapple, chopped
2 passionfruit
2 tablespoons chopped fresh mint
200 g (7 oz/heaped 3/4 cup) low-fat plain yoghurt
2 tablespoons sunflower seeds
2 tablespoons pepitas (pumpkin seeds)
2 tablespoons cashew nuts, chopped

Combine the papaya, pineapple, passionfruit and mint. Divide between two serving bowls. Dollop over the yoghurt and sprinkle over the seeds and cashew nuts.

Japanese-style scrambled eggs

Serves 1

1/2 onion, finely diced
1 garlic clove, crushed
100 g (31/2 oz) shiitake mushrooms
10 g (1/4 oz) shredded nori (see Note)
1 egg
5 egg whites
1 teaspoon tamari soy sauce, to serve

Fry the onion and garlic with a little water until golden. Add the shiitake mushrooms and cook until heated through. Set aside and keep warm.

Beat the egg and egg whites with 2 tablespoons water, the nori and some freshly ground black pepper.

Heat a non-stick frying pan over medium heat and spray with a little olive oil. Add the egg mixture. Cook, stirring the eggs with a wooden spoon or spatula, until the eggs are lightly set. The finished texture should be fluffy and moist. Serve immediately with the mushrooms and soy sauce on the side.

Note Nori is a Japanese seaweed that comes dried in packets. It is available in the Asian or health food section of most supermarkets.

Smashed berry pancakes

Makes 12

60 g (2¹/₄ oz/¹/₂ cup) soy flour
60 g (2¹/₄ oz/¹/₂ cup) natural or vanilla protein
   powder
3 tablespoons low-kilojoule sweetener
2 teaspoons baking powder
1 teaspoon ground cinnamon
¹/₂ teaspoon natural almond extract
2 teaspoons natural vanilla extract
125 ml (4 fl oz/¹/₂ cup) skim milk
2 eggs or 4 egg whites
1 small apple, grated

Smashed berry compote
300 g (10¹/₂ oz) raspberries
1 tablespoon honey or maple syrup
60 ml (2 fl oz/¹/₄ cup) orange juice
250 g (9 oz/1²/₃ cups) strawberries, halved
150 g (5¹/₂ oz/1 cup) blueberries

Combine the flour, protein powder, sweetener, baking powder, cinnamon, almond and vanilla extracts, milk, eggs and apple in a bowl.

Heat a non-stick frying pan over medium-low heat and lightly spray with a little oil. Spoon large spoonfuls of batter into the pan, 1 or 2 at a time. Cook until golden on both sides.

For the compote, smash the raspberries with a fork, then stir in the honey and orange juice. Fold in the other strawberries and blueberries. Spoon over the pancakes and serve.

Fried egg whites with cheese and tomato

Serves 1

6 egg whites
1 tomato, sliced
20 g (³/₄ oz) low-fat cheese, grated
chopped fresh basil, to garnish (optional)

Whisk the egg whites for 1 minute until fluffy.

Heat a non-stick frying pan over medium heat and spray with a little olive oil. Add the beaten egg whites, then reduce the heat and allow the base of the egg whites to brown and set.

Add the tomato and cheese and season with freshly ground black pepper. Place under a hot grill (broiler) for 1 minute, or until the top is set and the cheese is golden. Garnish with chopped basil, if using, and serve.

Raw energy fruit smoothies

In the mornings, I often pull out the blender and whizz up a yummy fresh fruit smoothie for my breakfast. The following are a few of my favourite recipes. They're all a convenient way of getting a nourishing vitamin and energy hit.

Banana and blueberry smoothie

Serves 1

125 ml (4 fl oz/^{1}/$_2$ cup) low-fat milk or soy milk
1 small banana
80 g (2^3/$_4$ oz/^{1}/$_2$ cup) frozen blueberries
2 heaped tablespoons natural or vanilla protein
   powder

Combine the ingredients in a blender with 125 ml (4 fl oz/^{1}/$_2$ cup) water. Blend until smooth and creamy. Serve immediately.

Red papaya and strawberry smoothie

Serves 1

^{1}/$_2$ small red papaya, seeded and chopped
125 ml (4 fl oz/^{1}/$_2$ cup) apple juice
250 g (9 oz/1^2/$_3$ cups) strawberries, halved
100 g (3^1/$_2$ oz) silken tofu
crushed ice, to blend

Combine the ingredients in a blender. Blend until smooth. Serve immediately.

Mango, passionfruit and yoghurt smoothie

Serves 1

1 mango, chopped
pulp from 2 passionfruit
200 g (7 oz/heaped 3/4 cup) low-fat plain yoghurt with
   live cultures
pinch of ground cardamom
pinch of ground cinnamon
crushed ice, to blend

Combine the ingredients in a blender with 125 ml (4 fl oz/
1/2 cup) water. Blend until smooth. Serve immediately.

Strawberry power smoothie

Serves 1

250 g (9 oz/12/3 cups) strawberries, halved
125 ml (4 fl oz/1/2 cup) chilled low-fat milk or soy milk
2 tablespoons natural or vanilla protein powder
crushed ice, to blend

Combine the ingredients in a blender. Blend until smooth.
Serve immediately.

Note Protein powder is available in supermarkets or
health food stores. A few scoops add a good protein
boost to breakfast smoothies. Make sure to choose a
vanilla or neutral-based natural powder that is low in
sugar and fat. The protein will fill you up and keep you in
power mode for the whole morning.

Fresh figs with pink grapefruit and honey

Serves 1

1 pink grapefruit
3 figs, halved
1 tablespoon chopped pistachio nuts
1 teaspoon honey

Peel the grapefruit. Remove the segments and put into a serving bowl. Arrange the halved figs over the top. Sprinkle over the nuts and drizzle with the honey.

Note When you have a little extra time on your hands, try grilled (broiled) figs in honey and cinnamon. Spread a teaspoon of honey onto halved figs and dust with a little ground cinnamon. Grill (broil) for about 3 minutes, or until warmed through. Put on top of the grapefruit segments, as in the above recipe, then dollop with some low-fat plain yoghurt and sprinkle with chopped pistachio nuts.

Papaya topped with berries and passionfruit

Serves 1

1 small red papaya
150 g (5^1/2 oz/1 cup) strawberries, raspberries or
  blueberries
pulp from 2 passionfruit
100 g (3^1/2 oz/heaped ^{1}/3 cup) low-fat plain yoghurt
  or 50 g (1^3/4 oz/heaped ^{1}/4 cup) cottage cheese,
  to serve

Cut the papaya in half lengthways and remove the seeds. Fill the papaya halves with the berries and spoon over the passionfruit pulp. Serve with yoghurt or cottage cheese.

Note I also like to do the same with a chilled honeydew melon or rockmelon using fresh blueberries, low-fat vanilla yoghurt and a handful of raw almonds.

Toast toppers

This selection of toast toppers makes a quick and delicious healthy breakfast. For those with wheat and gluten allergies, select appropriate bread.

Creamy scrambled eggs on toast

Serves 1

1 egg
5 egg whites
1 tablespoon chopped chives or sage
1 slice wholemeal (whole-wheat) or rye sourdough
  bread
1 tablespoon low-fat ricotta cheese

Beat the egg and egg whites in a bowl with the herbs. Pour into a medium–hot non-stick frying pan sprayed with a little olive oil. Cook over gentle heat, until soft and creamy. Meanwhile, toast the bread. Remove the eggs from the heat and fold through the ricotta. Pile over the toast, grind over a little black pepper and serve.

Mushrooms, spinach and ricotta on toast

Serves 1

1 garlic clove, crushed
1/2 red onion, sliced
150 g (5 1/2 oz) mushrooms, quartered
1 handful baby English spinach leaves
1 teaspoon chopped oregano
1 slice wholegrain or rye sourdough bread
50 g (1 3/4 oz/scant 1/4 cup) low-fat ricotta cheese

Fry the garlic, onion and mushrooms in a non-stick pan until golden, using a little water to help with the cooking. Add the spinach leaves and oregano. Toss through until the spinach has wilted. Toast the bread, then spread with the ricotta. Pile over the mushroom mixture and serve.

Sardines with tomato and spinach on toast

Serves 1

1 slice wholemeal (whole-wheat) or rye bread
1 small handful baby English spinach or rocket
  (arugula) leaves
100 g (3¹/2 oz) tinned sardines in spring water
1 tomato, sliced, or 4 cherry tomatoes, halved

Toast the bread. Top with the spinach or rocket, sardines and tomato. Grind over a little black pepper and serve.

Note Cooked fresh sardines can be used in place of the tinned variety, if you have time. Just sauté quickly in a non-stick frying pan with 1 teaspoon olive oil. Drizzle with lemon juice and sprinkle with 1 tablespoon chopped parsley and freshly ground black pepper.

Rye with hummus and tomato

Serves 1

2 slices dark rye sourdough bread
2 tablespoons hummus
1 handful baby English spinach or rocket (arugula)
  leaves
1 tomato, sliced

Toast the bread and spread with the hummus. Top with the spinach and the tomato. Grind over black pepper and serve.

Tuna fritters

Serves 1–2

185 g (6¹/₂ oz) tin tuna in spring water, drained
1 egg or 2 egg whites
1 spring onion (scallion), sliced
30 g (1 oz/¹/₂ cup) fresh soya beans (optional)
2 teaspoons oyster or sweet chilli sauce (optional)

Combine the tuna, egg or egg whites, spring onion and soya beans, if using, then season with freshly ground black pepper.

Heat a non-stick frying pan over medium heat and spray lightly with a little olive oil. Place spoonfuls of the tuna mixture into the pan, flatten them slightly and cook for 3 minutes each side, or until golden and cooked through. Serve immediately and top with a little oyster or sweet chilli sauce, if using.

Note These fritters are delicious accompanied with some sautéed shiitake mushrooms. Vegetarians can make tasty fritters using firm tofu. Put in a food processor 600 g (1 lb 5 oz/3¹/₄ cups) cubed firm tofu, 2 egg whites and 2 teaspoons red curry paste and process until smooth. Mix with the rest of the ingredients and pepper to taste and form into patties. Lightly coat the patties with ground almonds or a little rice flour and cook until heated through and golden on both sides.

Smoked salmon with baby spinach and soft poached egg

Serves 1

2 large handfuls baby English spinach leaves, washed
1 tomato, cut into wedges
100 g (3¹/₂ oz) sliced smoked salmon
1 egg
2 tablespoons shaved parmesan cheese

Combine the spinach leaves, tomato and salmon in a serving bowl. Fill a small saucepan with water and add a splash of lemon juice or vinegar. Boil, then reduce the heat to very low.

Add the egg and simmer for 3 minutes, or until softly poached. Remove from the water with a slotted spoon. Place the poached egg on top of the leaves and salmon and garnish with the cheese. Serve immediately.

Spiced basmati rice porridge with red papaya and pistachio nuts

Serves 4

200 g (7 oz/1 cup) basmati rice
500 ml (17 fl oz/ 2 cups) low-fat milk
1/2 teaspoon ground cinnamon
1/4 teaspoon ground cardamom
zest from 1 orange
2 tablespoons honey
2 teaspoons natural vanilla extract
50 g (13/4 oz) dried apricots, chopped
50 g (13/4 oz) sultanas (golden raisins)
1 small red papaya, seeded and chopped
50 g (13/4 oz/1/3 cup) pistachio nuts, chopped

Combine the rice, milk, cinnamon, cardamom, orange zest, honey and vanilla in a saucepan with 500 ml (17 fl oz/2 cups) water. Boil, then cover and reduce the heat to low. Simmer for about 30 minutes, stirring occasionally until most of the liquid has been absorbed and the rice is creamy. Add the apricots and sultanas and stir through. Serve in bowls, topped with the chopped papaya and pistachio nuts.

Notes Other fruit, such as sliced banana, blueberries, orange segments or passionfruit, can be used in place of the papaya.

The rice porridge can be made in advance (add the papaya and pistachios just before serving). It keeps well in the refrigerator for up to 3 days and reheats well. It can be eaten hot or cold.

Banana and blueberry stuffed French toast

Serves 2

4 egg whites
60 ml (2 fl oz/1/4 cup) low-fat milk or soy milk
2 teaspoons natural vanilla extract
4 slices good-quality wholegrain sourdough fruit
  bread
2 tablespoons low-fat ricotta or cottage cheese
2 small bananas, smashed
1/2 teaspoon ground cinnamon
125 g (41/2 oz/heaped 3/4 cup) blueberries

Combine the egg whites, milk and vanilla in a bowl. Dip both sides of the bread into the egg mixture for a few seconds. Transfer the bread to a hot non-stick frying pan sprayed with a little vegetable oil. Cook over medium heat until golden and crisp on both sides.

Place one slice of the French toast onto each of two serving plates. Top with the ricotta or cottage cheese, banana, cinnamon and blueberries. Sandwich with the other pieces of French toast and serve.

Note French toast can also be cooked in a jaffle maker. Make a sandwich from the bread, cottage cheese, banana, cinnamon and blueberries. Briefly coat in the egg mix and cook in a preheated jaffle maker until golden
.

Nourishing miso soup with rice and silken tofu

Serves 2

100 g (3½ oz/½ cup) brown rice or basmati rice
500 ml (17 fl oz/2 cups) vegetable stock
1 tablespoon grated fresh ginger
1 tablespoon white miso paste, or to taste
300 g (10½ oz) silken tofu, sliced
1 spring onion (scallion), sliced, to garnish
1 sliced red chilli (optional)

Combine the rice and 375 ml (13 fl oz/1½ cups) water in a saucepan. Bring to the boil, then reduce the heat and cover with a tight-fitting lid. Cook for 30–40 minutes, or until all the water has been absorbed. Turn off the heat and allow to sit for a further 10 minutes.

Combine the stock and ginger in another saucepan and heat. Mix a little of the stock with the miso paste to dissolve it and then add the paste to the rest of the liquid. Do not let it boil. Check for taste and add more miso if necessary. Divide the warm rice and sliced tofu between two serving bowls. Spoon over the hot miso stock. Garnish with the spring onion and chilli, if using, and serve.

Notes Miso is a fermented soya bean paste available from the Asian and health food sections in your supermarket. For this recipe use shiro miso, which is a mild-tasting white miso paste made from rice and soya beans. It can also be used to flavour soups, stews, sauces and dressings.

Other ingredients can be added to the stock, such as vegetables like bok choy (pak choy), English spinach, sweet corn and mushrooms. You can also add 1 tablespoon wakame seaweed. It needs to simmer for 3 minutes before serving.

Sweet corn and bean succotash

Serves 2

1 red onion, finely diced
175 g (6 oz/1 cup) sweet corn kernels
1 red capsicum (pepper), diced
200 g (7 oz) tinned red kidney beans, drained
1 chilli, seeded and chopped (optional)
2 tomatoes, diced
1/4 teaspoon ground cumin
juice from 1 lime
2 spring onions (scallions), sliced
1 handful chopped coriander (cilantro) leaves
1/2 avocado, sliced

Fry the onion in a little water or vegetable stock until golden. Add the sweet corn, capsicum, beans, chilli, tomato, cumin and some freshly ground black pepper. Cook for 2–3 minutes until heated through, adding a little water or stock when necessary to prevent sticking.

Remove the pan from the heat and add the lime juice, then the spring onion and coriander. Divide between two bowls and top each serving with avocado slices.

Vanilla and cinnamon poached stone fruits

Serves 6

1 kg (2 lb 4 oz) mixed stone fruits, such as freestone
  peaches, apricots, plums, nectarines and cherries
750 ml (26 fl oz/3 cups) apple juice
2 cinnamon sticks
1 vanilla bean, split lengthways
600 g (1 lb 5 oz/2 1/3 cups) low-fat plain yoghurt

Bring a large saucepan of water to the boil. Prepare a bowl of iced water. Plunge all the fruit, except the cherries, into the boiling water for about 1 minute, then remove with a slotted spoon and transfer to the bowl of iced water. Remove from the water and peel away the skins. Cut the fruit in half and remove the stones, if you want, or leave them whole.

Combine the apple juice, cinnamon and vanilla bean in a separate saucepan and heat until just boiling. Add the fruit, except for the cherries, and simmer over low heat for about 5 minutes. Remove the pan from the heat and add the cherries. Cool slightly, then serve warm with the yoghurt (or allow to cool completely).

Note Peeling the fruit is optional; it will look nicer if you do so. The poached fruit keeps for about 4 days covered in the refrigerator.

Warm salmon kedgeree

Serves 4–6

1 onion, finely diced
1 cinnamon stick
1/4 teaspoon ground coriander
1/4 teaspoon ground turmeric
200 g (7 oz/1 cup) basmati rice
375 ml (13 fl oz/11/2 cups) chicken stock
1 red capsicum (pepper), diced
100 g (31/2 oz/1/2 cup) fresh or frozen sweet corn
    kernels
100 g (31/2 oz/2/3 cup) green peas
2 handfuls baby English spinach leaves
splash of fish sauce
juice from 1/2 lime
300 g (101/2 oz) poached salmon fillet or tinned red
    salmon
4 hard-boiled eggs, whites roughly chopped (yolks
    not used)
2 tablespoons chopped coriander (cilantro) leaves

Sauté the onion with the spices in a pan with a little water
until golden. Add the rice, stock, capsicum, corn and
peas. Boil, then cover and reduce the heat and simmer
for 12–15 minutes. Fold through the spinach leaves, turn
off the heat and allow to sit for a further 5 minutes. Add the
fish sauce, lime juice, salmon, chopped egg whites and
coriander. Stir through and serve hot or cold.

Note Vegetarians can use brown lentils or chickpeas in
place of the salmon, and vegetable stock in place of the
chicken stock.

Asian-style fried eggs with silken tofu and mushrooms

Serves 1

100 g (31/2 oz) mushrooms, sliced
1 egg
5 egg whites
1 teaspoon grated fresh ginger
100 g (31/2 oz) silken tofu, sliced
1 teaspoon oyster sauce (see Note)
1 spring onion (scallion), sliced
1 red chilli, sliced (optional)

Preheat the grill (broiler). Cook the mushrooms until
golden in a hot non-stick frying pan, adding a little stock
or water to stop them sticking.

Beat the egg, egg whites, ginger and some freshly
ground black pepper until combined. Pour into the
cleaned, hot non-stick frying pan sprayed with a little olive
oil. Cook over medium heat until the eggs have just set
and the underside is just golden. Place the tofu over the
top of the eggs and finish cooking them under the hot grill
until set. Slide the eggs onto a serving plate and top with
the mushrooms, oyster sauce, spring onion and chilli.

Note Sweet chilli sauce or soy sauce can be used in
place of the oyster sauce.

Power porridge

Serves 1

30 g (1 oz/$^{1}/_{4}$ cup) rice bran
25 g (1 oz/$^{1}/_{4}$ cup) LSA (ground linseeds (flax seed),
　　sunflower seed and almonds)
1 apple or pear, grated with the skin on
60 ml (2 fl oz/$^{1}/_{4}$ cup) apple juice
60 ml (2 fl oz/$^{1}/_{4}$ cup) low-fat milk or soy milk
pinch of ground cinnamon
1 small banana, sliced

Combine the rice bran, LSA, grated apple or pear, apple
juice, milk and cinnamon in a small saucepan. Stir over
medium heat for 3 minutes, or until heated through and
the mixture is creamy. Add more water or milk if needed.
Pour into a serving bowl and top with the sliced banana.

Pink grapefruit and strawberry salad

Serves 1

250 g (9 oz/1$^{2}/_{3}$ cups) strawberries, halved
2 pink grapefruit, sliced
1 tablespoon chopped mint
$^{1}/_{2}$ teaspoon grated fresh ginger
1 teaspoon natural vanilla extract
1 teaspoon honey
1 small handful raw cashew nuts

Combine the strawberries, grapefruit, mint, ginger, vanilla
and honey in a serving bowl. Sprinkle with the cashew
nuts and serve.

Grilled summer peaches with raspberries

Serves 1

2 freestone peaches, halved and stoned
1 teaspoon honey
1/4 teaspoon ground cinnamon
3 tablespoons low-fat plain yoghurt
85 g (3 oz/2/3 cup) raspberries

Preheat the grill (broiler). Arrange the peach halves on a baking tray lined with foil. Drizzle over the honey and sprinkle with the cinnamon. Grill (broil) for 2–3 minutes, or until warm and sizzling. Dollop the yoghurt into a serving dish and arrange the peaches over the top. Scatter with the raspberries and serve.

Scrambled tofu with broccoli

Serves 1

1/2 onion, finely diced
1 garlic clove, crushed
1 red chilli, seeded and sliced
1/2 head broccoli, finely chopped
60 ml (2 fl oz/1/4 cup) vegetable stock
150 g (51/2 oz/3/4 cup) firm tofu, lightly mashed
2 tablespoons chopped coriander (cilantro) leaves
1–2 teaspoons tamari soy sauce

Heat a non-stick pan over medium heat. Add the onion, garlic, chilli, broccoli and stock. Cook until the broccoli is just tender and the liquid has evaporated, adding more stock or water if necessary to help cook the broccoli. Stir in the tofu, coriander and soy sauce. Cook briefly, to heat through, and serve.

Tuna, tomato and avocado melts

Serves 1

1 slice rye or wholemeal (whole-wheat) sourdough
  bread
100 g (3^1/$_2$ oz) tinned tuna in spring water, drained
1 tomato, diced
^{1}/$_4$ avocado, mashed
20 g (^{3}/$_4$ oz) low-fat cheese, grated

Preheat the grill (broiler) to high. Toast or grill (broil) the
bread lightly on both sides. Combine the tuna, tomato
and avocado, then spread over the toast. Sprinkle over
the cheese. Place under the grill to melt and serve.

Breakfast pear and passionfruit crumble

Serves 4

6 pears, peeled, cored and diced
2 tablespoons honey
juice from 2 limes
pulp from 4 passionfruit
400 g (14 oz/1^2/$_3$ cups) low-fat plain yoghurt
150 g (6 oz/1 cup) honey-toasted muesli with
  almonds, sultanas, apple and apricot (see page 71)

Put the diced pears, honey and lime juice in a saucepan.
Cook over medium heat until the pears are soft. Remove
the pan from the heat and fold through the passionfruit.
Spoon into serving dishes and top with the yoghurt and
muesli. The pears can be served warm or cold.

Note Other fruits can be used in place of the pears. Try
apple and cinnamon, or mixed berries without the lime.

Organic fruit and nut spelt bread

Makes 2 loaves

625 g (1 lb 6 oz/5 cups) spelt flour
2 teaspoons baking powder
1 teaspoon ground cinnamon
1 teaspoon ground ginger
1/4 teaspoon ground cloves
1/4 teaspoon ground nutmeg
1 teaspoon sea salt
15 g (1/2 oz) dried yeast or 30 g (1 oz) fresh yeast
50 g (1 3/4 oz) honey

2 teaspoons natural vanilla extract
zest from 2 oranges
2 tablespoons macadamia nut oil or grapeseed oil
600 g (1 lb 5 oz) chopped dried fruits, such as
    apricots, pears, figs, sultanas, dates
150 g (5 1/2 oz) walnuts, chopped
1 egg, lightly beaten
2 tablespoons low-fat milk

Combine the flour, baking powder, spices, salt and yeast in a large bowl. In a separate bowl, combine the honey, vanilla, orange zest and oil with 370 ml (13 fl oz) warm water. Pour the wet ingredients into the flour and mix well to form a dough. Knead for about 10 minutes, or until the dough is smooth and elastic.

Place the dough into a large bowl and cover with plastic wrap. Leave in a warm place for 1–1 1/2 hours until it has doubled in size. Knead the dried fruit and walnuts into the dough until all mixed through. Shape into two free-form loaves and place onto a baking tray lined with baking paper. Leave to rise in a warm place for 1 hour. Preheat the oven to 200°C (400°F/Gas 6).

Using a pastry brush, lightly brush the loaves with the combined egg and milk. Bake the loaves for 20 minutes, then reduce the heat to 180°C (350°F/Gas 4) and bake for another 20 minutes. Cover the tops with foil if necessary to prevent overbrowning. Allow to cool before serving.

Serve 1–2 slices per person, either as they are or toasted. Top with low-fat ricotta cheese and strawberries, cottage cheese and banana, sugar-free jam, honey or tahini.

LUNCH

Chicken and pineapple coleslaw

Serves 1

100 g (3¹/2 oz) lean grilled or poached chicken breast
1 carrot, grated
150 g (5¹/2 oz/2 cups) thinly sliced savoy cabbage
100 g (3¹/2 oz/¹/2 cup) chopped pineapple
1 spring onion (scallion), sliced
2 tablespoons chopped coriander (cilantro) leaves
   or Vietnamese mint
2 tablespoons chopped mint

Coconut lime dressing

60 ml (2 fl oz/¹/4 cup) low-fat coconut milk
juice from 2 limes
2 tablespoons fish sauce
1 teaspoon honey or soft brown sugar

Shred the chicken. Combine the chicken with the carrot, cabbage, pineapple, spring onion, coriander and mint.

Mix together the dressing ingredients and taste for seasoning. Adjust to taste if necessary. Pour over the salad and mix well. Serve in bowls.

Note This dish is delicious with king prawns (shrimp), steamed white fish or crab. Vegetarians can replace the chicken with soya beans or firm shredded tofu.

Chicken and prawn salad with avocado, mango and chilli sauce

Serves 2

¹/4 iceberg lettuce, shredded
1 small handful mint, chopped
1 handful coriander (cilantro) leaves, chopped
200 g (7 oz) chicken breast, poached and sliced
200 g (7 oz) king prawns (shrimp), cooked and
   peeled with tails intact
¹/2 avocado, sliced
¹/2 mango, sliced
60 ml (2 fl oz/¹/4 cup) lime juice
80 ml (2¹/2 fl oz/¹/3 cup) sweet chilli sauce

Combine the lettuce, mint and coriander and divide between two serving bowls. On top, arrange the chicken, prawns, avocado and mango. Drizzle over the lime juice and top with the sweet chilli sauce.

Greek salad with tuna and balsamic dressing

Serves 1

100 g (3¹/₂ oz) tinned tuna in spring water, drained
1 tablespoon chopped fresh oregano or 1 teaspoon
  dried oregano
2 Lebanese (short) cucumbers, sliced
2 tomatoes, cut into wedges
30 g (1 oz/¹/₄ cup) crumbled low-fat feta cheese
4 black olives, pitted and chopped
balsamic vinegar, to serve

Combine the tuna, oregano, cucumber, tomato, feta and olives in a serving bowl. Drizzle over a little balsamic vinegar before serving.

Note Grilled (broiled) tuna steaks can be used in place of the tinned tuna. Vegetarians can substitute the tuna with broad (fava) beans.

Smoked salmon and lettuce wraps

Serves 1

¹/₂ butter lettuce, leaves separated
100 g (3¹/₂ oz) sliced smoked salmon
2 hard-boiled eggs, halved and yolks discarded
50 g (1³/₄ oz) bean sprouts
1 handful mint
1 handful coriander (cilantro) or Thai basil leaves
1 tablespoon sweet chilli sauce

Arrange the lettuce leaves on a serving plate. Fill each leaf with a little of the smoked salmon, cooked egg white, bean shoots and herbs. Roll up, then dip into the sweet chilli sauce.

Note Poached or tinned salmon, prawns (shrimp) or chicken can be used in place of the smoked salmon. Vegetarians can use finely grated tofu or soya beans.

Chicken salad with honey mustard dressing

Serves 1

100 g (3$^{1}/_{2}$ oz) poached chicken breast, shredded
2 large handfuls salad leaves or $^{1}/_{2}$ a butter lettuce, washed and torn
1 tomato, sliced
$^{1}/_{4}$ red onion, sliced

Honey mustard dressing
1 teaspoon dijon mustard
1 teaspoon honey
80 ml (2$^{1}/_{2}$ fl oz/$^{1}/_{3}$ cup) balsamic vinegar

Combine the chicken, salad leaves, tomato and onion in a bowl. Mix the dressing ingredients together and toss through the salad.

Note For a vegetarian meal substitute grated firm tofu for the chicken. King prawns (shrimp) or poached salmon are also lovely in this salad.

Guacamole with crunchy vegetables

Serves 4

300 g (10$^{1}/_{2}$ oz) silken tofu, drained
$^{1}/_{2}$ avocado
1 garlic clove, crushed
juice from $^{1}/_{2}$ lemon
2 tablespoons chopped coriander (cilantro) leaves
$^{1}/_{4}$ teaspoon ground cumin

A selection of raw crunchy vegetables, such as carrot, capsicum (pepper), zucchini (courgette), mushrooms, celery, cherry tomatoes, asparagus, baby corn, or witlof (chicory/Belgian endive) leaves

Combine the tofu and avocado in a food processor and process until smooth. Fold in the garlic, lemon juice, coriander, cumin and some freshly ground black pepper. Serve with a selection of crunchy vegetables.

Note This dip makes a delicious snack and will keep for about 3 days, covered, in the refrigerator. It's great in sandwiches and burgers and as an accompaniment to warm steamed vegetables, chicken or fish.

Steamed white fish with mango relish

Serves 4

Mango relish
1 red onion, finely diced
1 large mango, diced
2 teaspoons grated fresh ginger
60 ml (2 fl oz/1/4 cup) sweet chilli sauce
juice and zest from 1 lime
2 tablespoons chopped coriander (cilantro) leaves

4 x 150 g (51/2 oz) pieces firm white fish fillets, such
   as blue eye cod
2 telegraph (long) cucumbers, sliced into ribbons,
   to serve

To make the mango relish, combine the onion, mango, ginger, chilli sauce, lime juice and coriander in a bowl.

Steam the fish in a steamer for 8–10 minutes, or until cooked. Arrange the cucumber ribbons on plates and place the fish alongside. Top the fish with the mango relish and serve.

Note The fish can also be pan-fried in a non-stick pan sprayed with a little olive oil, or poached in chicken stock.

Spinach and ricotta mushroom pizzas

Serves 1

1 tablespoon pine nuts
2–3 large field mushrooms
2 teaspoons tomato paste (concentrated purée)
1 handful baby English spinach leaves, shredded
pinch of ground nutmeg
90 g (31/4 oz/1/4 cup) low-fat ricotta cheese
1 teaspoon fresh oregano
1 tomato, quartered, or 8 cherry tomatoes, halved
1 large handful rocket (arugula)

Preheat the oven to 220°C (425°F/Gas 7). Toast the pine nuts in a small non-stick frying pan over medium heat until golden.

Place the mushrooms, stem side up, on a baking tray and spread with the tomato paste. Combine the spinach, nutmeg, ricotta, pine nuts, oregano and some freshly ground black pepper. Spoon the mixture into the mushrooms and top with the tomato. Bake for 15 minutes, or until heated through. Arrange the rocket on a serving plate. Top with the baked mushroom pizzas and serve immediately.

Creamy carrot soup

Serves 4

1 leek, sliced
1 onion, chopped
1 teaspoon grated fresh ginger
1 litre (35 fl oz/4 cups) vegetable stock
500 g (1 lb 2 oz) carrots, cut into small chunks
low-fat plain yoghurt, to garnish
chopped chives, to garnish

Combine the leek, onion, ginger, stock and carrots in a saucepan. Bring to the boil, then cook over medium-low heat for about 20 minutes, or until the carrots are tender.

Remove the saucepan from the heat and cool the soup slightly. Blend the soup in a blender or hand-held blender until it is smooth. Season with freshly ground black pepper. Return the soup to the pan and place back on the stovetop to heat through. Pour into bowls and garnish with a dollop of yoghurt and some chives before serving.

Note You can add 60 g (2¼ oz/1 cup) fresh soya beans to the soup if you like, for extra protein.

Baked stuffed potato with spinach and ricotta

Serves 2

2 large potatoes
100 g (3½ oz) English spinach or silverbeet (Swiss chard) leaves, blanched and chopped
150 g (5½ oz/scant ⅔ cup) low-fat ricotta or cottage cheese, plus extra, grated, to sprinkle
2 tablespoons tomato salsa, to serve

Preheat the oven to 180°C (350°F/Gas 4). Prick the skins of the potatoes and place onto a baking tray lined with foil or baking paper. Bake for about 40 minutes, or until soft. (You can also use the microwave and cook on HIGH for about 8–10 minutes.)

Cool slightly, then cut off the tops. Scoop out three-quarters of the flesh and put it into a bowl. Add the spinach, cheese and some freshly ground black pepper. Mix together well. Refill the potatoes with the mixture and sprinkle the tops with the extra grated cheese. Return the filled potatoes to the oven for a further 10 minutes to heat through. Serve with the tomato salsa on the side.

Barbecued chicken salad with mango yoghurt dressing

Serves 2

1 butter or baby cos (romaine) lettuce, torn into pieces
200 g (7 oz) skinless chicken breast from a
  barbecued chicken
1/2 red onion, sliced
12 cherry tomatoes, halved
1 handful almonds, to garnish (optional)

Mango yoghurt dressing
1/2 mango, diced
200 g (7 oz/heaped 3/4 cup) low-fat plain yoghurt
1 tablespoon lime juice
1 tablespoon chopped mint

Arrange the lettuce in a bowl. Top with the chicken, onion and tomato.

Make the mango yoghurt dressing by combining the mango, yoghurt and lime juice in a food processor. Process until smooth, then fold through the mint and a little freshly ground black pepper. Drizzle the dressing over the salad and top with the almonds.

Note Cooked turkey or prawns (shrimp) can also be used instead of the chicken. Vegetarians and vegans might like to use soya beans in place of the chicken, and silken tofu in the dressing instead of the yoghurt.

Soba noodle salad

Serves 2

120 g (4 oz) buckwheat or green tea soba noodles
50 g (1 3/4 oz/3/4 cup) bean sprouts, trimmed
2 spring onions (scallions), thinly sliced
25 g (1 oz/1/2 cup) snow pea (mangetout) sprouts,
  trimmed
6 shiitake mushrooms, sliced
100 g (3 1/2 oz) cooked crabmeat, flaked
1 teaspoon white sesame seeds, toasted

Dressing
2 tablespoons soy sauce
2 tablespoons mirin
1 garlic clove, crushed
1 teaspoon grated fresh ginger
1/4 teaspoon sesame oil

Cook the noodles in plenty of boiling water until tender. Drain and rinse under cold running water. Combine the noodles with the bean sprouts, spring onion, snow pea sprouts, mushroom, crabmeat and sesame seeds.

Mix together the dressing ingredients and pour over the salad. Toss through and divide between serving plates.

Note Steamed and flaked firm white fish fillet or chicken breast can be used in place of the crabmeat. Vegetarians can use grated firm tofu or shelled green soya beans.

Sweet corn fritters with mushrooms, spinach and tomato

Serves 4

3 cobs of fresh corn, kernels removed (this will give
    you about 325 g/11^1/2 oz/1^2/3 cups)
2 tablespoons chopped coriander (cilantro) leaves
2 spring onions (scallions), chopped
4 egg whites
2–3 tablespoons unbleached plain (all-purpose) flour
1/2 teaspoon baking powder
50 g (2 oz) baby English spinach leaves
4 large field mushrooms, grilled (broiled)
4 roma (plum) tomatoes, halved and grilled (broiled)
soy sauce or sweet chilli sauce, to serve

Combine the corn kernels, coriander, spring onion, egg whites, flour, baking powder and some freshly ground black pepper. Mix to form a chunky pancake mixture. Heat a non-stick frying pan over medium heat and spray with olive oil. For each fritter, dollop 2 tablespoons of mixture in the pan, flattening out slightly with the back of the spoon. Cook in batches over medium heat for 3–4 minutes on each side, or until crisp and golden.

Serve stacked on a bed of spinach leaves with the mushrooms and tomato alongside. Accompany with a little soy sauce or sweet chilli sauce on the side.

Cool gazpacho

Serves 2

375 ml (13 fl oz/1^1/2 cups) low-sodium tomato
    juice, chilled
200 g (7 oz) tin red kidney or adzuki beans, drained
2 roma (plum) tomatoes, peeled and diced
2 Lebanese (short) cucumbers, sliced
125 g (4^1/2 oz) cherry tomatoes, halved
1 yellow capsicum (pepper), diced
1/4 red onion, finely diced
1 handful coriander (cilantro) leaves, chopped
dash of Tabasco sauce
1 garlic clove, crushed
1/2 avocado, diced
juice of 1/2 lime

Combine the tomato juice, beans, roma tomato, cucumber, cherry tomato, capsicum, onion, coriander, Tabasco, garlic and some freshly ground black pepper. Divide between serving bowls and spoon over the combined avocado and lime juice.

Note This soup can be garnished with crabmeat, large prawns (shrimp) or steamed mussels. It keeps in the refrigerator for a couple of days and makes a great quick meal for lunch or dinner. Serve cool from the refrigerator or, if you want a hot soup, just heat up and enjoy with a dollop of low-fat sour cream or yoghurt.

Bolognaise sauce

Serves 6

500 g (1 lb 2 oz) minced (ground) lean beef
   topside or veal
1 onion, diced
2 garlic cloves, chopped
1 large carrot, grated
1 celery stalk, finely diced
500 ml (17 fl oz/2 cups) beef or chicken stock

800 g (1 lb 12 oz) tinned chopped peeled tomatoes
2 tablespoons tomato paste (concentrated purée)
2 teaspoons soft brown sugar
spaghetti, to serve
1 handful flat-leaf (Italian) parsley, chopped, to serve
2 tablespoons freshly shaved parmesan cheese,
   to taste

Sauté the mince in a hot non-stick saucepan until brown. Add 500 ml (17 fl oz/2 cups) boiling water and boil for 1 minute. Drain the mince in a colander to remove the extra saturated fat and return the mince to the pan. Add the onion, garlic, carrot, celery and stock. Cover and cook over medium heat for about 10 minutes. Add the tomato, tomato paste and sugar. Cook, uncovered, over medium heat for a further 15–20 minutes, or until the sauce is thick and rich. Cook the spaghetti or prepare the vegetable spaghetti (below). To serve, ladle the sauce over the spaghetti and garnish with parsley and parmesan.

If you want to serve your bolognaise with dried wheat spaghetti, use 500 g (1 lb 2 oz) for six people. Otherwise, you can make vegetable spaghetti. You will need about 8 large zucchini (courgettes). Slice them into fine spaghetti strands on a mandolin (available from kitchenware stores). Blanch in a saucepan of boiling water for 1 minute, then drain well and toss with a squeeze of lemon juice, 1 tablespoon olive oil, some chopped parsley and freshly ground black pepper.

To make a vegetarian bolognaise, put 1 diced onion, 2 chopped garlic cloves and 800 g (1 lb 12 oz) tinned chopped peeled tomatoes into a saucepan and simmer for 5–10 minutes. Add 400 g (14 oz) finely chopped mushrooms, 400 g (14 oz) tin kidney beans and 1 teaspoon oregano. Simmer for 20 minutes, then fold in a small handful chopped basil and season with a little freshly ground black pepper and sea salt. Serve over steamed seasonal vegetables or spaghetti, garnished with a light sprinkle of shaved parmesan cheese. Serves 6.

Brown rice salad with miso dressing

Serves 2

100 g (3¹/2 oz/³/4 cup) shiitake mushrooms, finely
   chopped
1 garlic clove, crushed
185 g (6¹/2 oz/1 cup) cooked brown rice (see Note)
400 g (14 oz) tin adzuki or soya beans
1 spring onion (scallion), sliced
2 Lebanese (short) cucumbers, finely diced
1 red capsicum (pepper), finely diced
1 sheet nori seaweed, finely shredded

Miso dressing

1 tablespoon white miso paste
1 tablespoon tahini
60 ml (2 fl oz/¹/4 cup) lime juice
1 tablespoon maple syrup

Sauté the shiitake mushroom and garlic in a hot non-stick frying pan, using a little water or stock to cook with. Remove from the heat and allow to cool.

Combine the mushrooms with the rice, beans, spring onion, cucumber, capsicum and seaweed. Mix the miso dressing ingredients together, adding a little water if necessary for a nice drizzling consistency. Pour over the salad and fold through. Serve warm or cold.

Note To cook the rice, put 100 g (3¹/2 oz/¹/2 cup) short-grain brown rice and 250 ml (9 fl oz/1 cup) water in a saucepan. Bring to the boil, then reduce the heat and cover. Cook for 40 minutes. Add a touch more water if necessary during cooking. Turn off the heat and allow to sit for 10 minutes, then remove the lid and allow to cool.

Soft rice paper rolls

Serves 2

2 garlic cloves, chopped
juice of 2 limes
2 tablespoons fish sauce
1 teaspoon soft brown sugar or shaved palm sugar
1 red capsicum (pepper), thinly sliced
2 handfuls baby English spinach leaves
1 large handful bean sprouts, trimmed
1 handful Vietnamese mint or coriander (cilantro)
   leaves, chopped
1 handful mint
200 g (7 oz) cooked and peeled prawns (shrimp),
   crabmeat or chicken breast, chopped
8 large rice paper sheets
sweet chilli sauce, to serve

Mix the garlic, lime juice, fish sauce and sugar together until combined. Add the rest of the salad ingredients and toss through well.

Soak a rice paper sheet in a bowl of hot water for about 30 seconds to soften, then lay on a work surface. Place a little pile of the salad ingredients in the centre of the rice paper sheet. Roll up the sheet, tucking in the edges halfway through rolling. Set aside while you make the remaining rolls. Serve with sweet chilli sauce.

Note Vegetarians can use grated firm tofu in place of the seafood or chicken.

Vegetable patties

Makes 12 patties

5 carrots
400 g (14 oz) tin chickpeas, rinsed and drained
370 g (13 oz/2 cups) cooked Japanese sushi rice or
   short-grain brown rice (see Note)
60 g (2¼ oz/¼ cup) tahini
2 spring onions (scallions), chopped
2 teaspoons miso paste
100 g (3½ oz) ground almonds (almond meal)
rice flour or sesame seeds, to coat (optional)

Steam the carrots until just tender. Allow to cool, then grate and set them aside.

Process the chickpeas in a food processor until broken up. Combine in a bowl with the grated carrot, rice, tahini, spring onion, miso and ground almonds. Form into patties and roll in the rice flour or sesame seeds, if using, then allow to set in the refrigerator for 30 minutes.

Heat a non-stick frying pan over medium heat and spray with a little olive oil. Cook the patties for 4–5 minutes on each side, or until golden. Serve hot or cold.

Note To cook the rice, put 220 g (7¾ oz/1 cup) short-grain sushi rice with 375 ml (13 fl oz/1½ cups) water in a saucepan. Bring to the boil, reduce heat and cover. Cook the rice for 20 minutes. Turn off the heat and allow to sit for a further 10 minutes. Remove the lid and allow to cool.

Sweet corn soup with crabmeat

Serves 4

1 onion, finely diced
1 garlic clove, crushed
1 tablespoon grated fresh ginger
1 lemon grass stem, finely chopped (white part only)
300 g (10½ oz/1½ cups) sweet corn kernels
1.5 litres (52 fl oz/6 cups) chicken stock
4 egg whites, beaten
250 g (9 oz) cooked crabmeat
2 spring onions (scallions), sliced
2 teaspoons soy sauce or tamari soy sauce, to season

Sauté the onion, garlic, ginger and lemon grass with a little water in a large saucepan over medium heat until softened. Add the corn kernels and stock, then simmer for about 10 minutes, or until the kernels are tender.

Add the egg whites in a thin stream, stirring the soup at the same time. Add the crabmeat, spring onion and soy sauce and cook for a further minute. Spoon into deep bowls and serve.

Note Cooked firm fish or prawns (shrimp) are a delicious substitute for the crabmeat. Vegetarians can use silken tofu instead of the crab.

Green papaya salad with chicken and prawns

Serves 2

2 small green papaya, seeded and grated
100 g (3½ oz) skinless chicken breast, poached and
  shredded
100 g (3½ oz) shelled and cooked king prawns
  (shrimp), sliced in half lengthways
1 carrot, finely grated
2 spring onions (scallions), sliced
1 handful Vietnamese mint or coriander (cilantro)
  leaves, chopped
1 handful mint, chopped
30 g (1 oz/scant ¼ cup) oven-roasted cashew nuts
  or almonds, chopped (optional)

Dressing
2 garlic cloves, crushed
juice from 4 limes
1 red chilli, sliced (optional)
80 ml (2½ fl oz/⅓ cup) fish sauce
2 teaspoons honey

Combine the green papaya, chicken, prawns, carrot,
spring onion and herbs. Make the dressing by mixing the
garlic, lime juice, chilli, fish sauce and honey. Pour the
dressing over the papaya salad and mix through. Divide
between serving plates. Garnish with the roasted nuts.

Chilli bean and guacamole lettuce wraps

Serves 4

400 g (14 oz) tin red kidney or adzuki beans, drained
1 green capsicum (pepper), finely diced
4 tomatoes, chopped, or 250 g (9 oz) cherry
  tomatoes, halved
2 spring onions (scallions), sliced
100 g (3½ oz) peeled raw broad beans
200 g (7 oz/1 cup) sweet corn kernels
1 teaspoon ground cumin
pinch of raw (demerara) sugar
1 red chilli, chopped

Guacamole
1 avocado, diced
1 tablespoon lime juice
2 tablespoons chopped parsley
2 tablespoons chopped coriander (cilantro) leaves

12 iceberg or butter lettuce leaves
50 g (1¾ oz/⅓ cup) grated low-fat cheese (optional)
sweet chilli sauce, to serve (optional)

Combine the beans, capsicum, tomato, spring onion,
corn kernels, broad beans, cumin, sugar and chilli. Make
the guacamole by combining the avocado, lime juice,
parsley and coriander. To assemble, fill the lettuce leaves
with a combination of bean mix, guacamole and then
some low-fat cheese. Serve with sweet chilli sauce.

Note The bean and guacamole mixtures are also good
served with warm wholemeal (whole-wheat) tortillas.

Thai fish cakes with cucumber, lime and sweet chilli sauce

Serves 4

500 g (1 lb 2 oz) firm white fish fillets, such as snapper or blue eye cod, chopped
1 egg white
2 tablespoons Thai red curry paste
2 tablespoons fish sauce
50 g (1^3/$_4$ oz) tinned water chestnuts, drained and chopped
^{1}/$_2$ red capsicum (pepper), diced
1 small handful coriander (cilantro) leaves, chopped
2 spring onions (scallions), finely chopped
2 limes
4 Lebanese (short) cucumbers, sliced, to serve
80 ml (2^1/$_2$ fl oz/^{1}/$_3$ cup) sweet chilli sauce, to serve

Combine the fish, egg white, curry paste and fish sauce in a food processor. Process until a paste forms. Transfer the fish mixture to a bowl and add the water chestnuts, capsicum, coriander and spring onion. Mix together and form into patties with wet hands. Allow to rest for 1 hour in the refrigerator before cooking. Heat a non-stick frying pan sprayed with olive oil and add the patties. Cook until golden on each side. Squeeze lime juice over the patties and serve with the cucumber and sweet chilli sauce.

Note For a vegetarian dish, combine 600 g (1 lb 5 oz) firm tofu with 2 egg whites and 2 teaspoons red curry paste in a food processor. Process until smooth. Mix with the rest of the ingredients and form into patties. Coat the patties lightly with ground almonds (almond meal) or a little rice flour and cook on both sides until crisp and golden.

Roasted Mediterranean vegetables with sardines, lemon and parsley

Serves 2

1 red capsicum (pepper), cut into chunks
200 g (7 oz) button mushrooms
4 roma (plum) tomatoes, quartered
2 zucchini (courgettes), cut into chunks
300 g (10 ^{1}/$_2$ oz) fresh uncooked sardines
juice of ^{1}/$_2$ lemon
1 garlic clove, crushed
1 tablespoon chopped flat-leaf (Italian) parsley
1 tablespoon cold-pressed olive oil or linseed oil

Preheat the oven to 220°C (425°F/Gas 7). Combine the capsicum, mushrooms, tomato and zucchini on a baking tray lined with foil or baking paper. Season with freshly ground black pepper. Roast for 25–30 minutes, or until the vegetables are soft. Tip the warm vegetables and any juices into a bowl.

Sauté the sardines quickly in a non-stick frying pan sprayed with a little olive oil. Squeeze the lemon and pour the juice over the vegetables. Add the sardines to the warm roasted vegetables along with the garlic, parsley and oil. Mix together lightly and serve. Eat warm or cold.

Note Tinned or fresh tuna can be used in place of the sardines. Vegetarians can omit the sardines and use broad (fava) beans or cannellini beans instead.

The Sunday roast

Serves 4

1.5 kg (3 lb 5 oz) chicken
1 onion, sliced
4 garlic cloves, peeled
4 slices fresh ginger
1 tablespoon honey
2 tablespoons fish sauce
1 lemon grass stem, chopped (white part only)

Basting mix

250 ml (9 fl oz/1 cup) chicken stock
2 tablespoons soy sauce
80 ml (2^1/$_2$ fl oz/^{1}/$_3$ cup) mirin

4 potatoes, peeled and halved
2 garlic cloves, crushed
1 tablespoon fish sauce
1 egg white
300 g (10^1/$_2$ oz) green beans, topped and tailed

Preheat the oven to 200°C (400°F/Gas 6). Wash and dry the chicken well. Combine the onion, garlic cloves, ginger, honey, fish sauce and lemon grass and stuff inside the chicken. Tie the legs together. Place the chicken, breast side up, on a roasting rack set in a roasting tin.

Combine all the basting mix ingredients. Cook the chicken for 1^1/$_4$ 1^1/$_2$ hours, basting it every 15 minutes until cooked. Check if the chicken is ready by piercing the thigh with a sharp knife — if the juices run clear it is ready.

Parboil the potatoes in a saucepan of boiling water for 5 minutes, then drain. Combine the garlic, fish sauce and egg white, then roll the potatoes in the mixture to cover. Place the potatoes onto a baking tray lined with baking paper and roast for 40 minutes, or until crisp and golden. Steam the beans until tender. Remove all the skin from the chicken and serve with the potatoes and beans.

Chicken burgers with macadamia nut and lemon

Serves 4

2 garlic cloves, crushed
2 spring onions (scallions), sliced
1 small handful coriander (cilantro) leaves, chopped
zest from 2 lemons
3 egg whites
500 g (1 lb 2 oz) minced (ground) lean chicken breast
50 g (1³/₄ oz/¹/₃ cup) roughly chopped macadamia nuts
100 g (3¹/₂ oz) tinned water chestnuts, drained and chopped

Combine all the ingredients in a bowl. Add freshly ground black pepper, to taste. Mix together well, then with wet hands form into small patties. Heat a non-stick frying pan and spray with a little olive oil. Cook over medium heat until the burgers are golden and cooked through. This should take 3–4 minutes on each side.

Note These burgers are delicious served hot or cold. They can be served with vegetables, a tossed salad or sandwiched between 2 slices wholegrain sourdough. Accompany with yoghurt mayonnaise (see page 123), oyster sauce or sweet chilli sauce for a complete meal.

Chunky vegetable soup

Serves 4

1 onion, diced
1 leek, sliced
2 garlic cloves, chopped
2 celery stalks, finely chopped
2 large carrots, diced
1 red capsicum (pepper), diced
1 yellow capsicum (pepper), diced
400 g (14 oz) tins crushed tomatoes
2 x 400 g (14 oz) tins mixed beans, drained
80 g (2³/₄ oz/¹/₂ cup) green peas
1 litre (35 fl oz/4 cups) vegetable stock
1 handful flat-leaf (Italian) parsley, chopped

Sauté the onion, leek and garlic with a little water in a large saucepan until soft. Add the celery, carrot and capsicum and cook for a few minutes. Add the tomato, beans, peas and stock. Simmer over low heat for 15 minutes, or until the vegetables are tender. Season with some freshly ground black pepper. Fold through the parsley just before serving. Ladle into serving bowls and enjoy.

Persian chickpea salad with orange and cinnamon dressing

Serves 2

400 g (14 oz) tin chickpeas, rinsed and drained
2 Lebanese (short) cucumbers, halved and sliced
2 tomatoes, chopped
1 small handful flat-leaf (Italian) parsley, chopped
1 small handful mint, chopped
1/2 red onion, sliced
50 g (1³/4 oz/1/3 cup) crumbled low-fat feta cheese
6 dried apricots, sliced
20 g (³/4 oz/1/4 cup) flaked almonds, toasted

Orange and cinnamon dressing
juice from 1/2 lemon
1 garlic clove, crushed
zest from 1 orange
1 teaspoon honey
1/2 teaspoon ground cumin
pinch of ground cinnamon

Combine the chickpeas, cucumber, tomato, parsley, mint, onion, feta, apricots and almonds in a bowl. Mix the dressing ingredients together and pour over the salad. Toss well and serve.

Salmon and vegetable frittatas

Makes 10 frittatas

2 eggs
10 egg whites
400 g (14 oz) tin red salmon
100 g (3¹/2 oz/1 bunch) English spinach, finely
  shredded
1 red capsicum (pepper), diced
90 g (3¹/4 oz/1/2 cup) sweet corn kernels
2 spring onions (scallions), sliced
100 g (3¹/2 oz/²/3 cup) cubed low-fat feta cheese

Preheat the oven to 180°C (350°F/Gas 4). Line 10 holes of a 12-hole muffin tin with paper cases. Beat together the eggs and egg whites and set aside. Combine the salmon, spinach, capsicum, corn kernels, spring onion, cheese and some freshly ground black pepper. Divide the mixture between the muffin cups. Fill the cups with the beaten egg mixture. Bake for 20–25 minutes, or until cooked and golden on top. Serve warm or cold.

Note For a vegetarian meal, replace the salmon with 300 g (10¹/2 oz/heaped 1¹/2 cups) chopped firm tofu or tempeh. The frittata can also be made in a large baking dish.

Zucchini spaghetti with avocado pesto

Serves 4

Avocado pesto

1 avocado, peeled and stoned
2 garlic cloves, crushed
juice from 3 limes
1 handful basil, roughly chopped
1 handful flat-leaf (Italian) parsley, chopped
40 g (1 1/2 oz/1/4 cup) pepitas (pumpkin seeds)
80 g (2 3/4 oz/1/2 cup) chopped almonds
1 teaspoon honey or apple juice concentrate

8 large zucchini (courgettes)
250 g (9 oz) cherry tomatoes
250 g (9 oz) yellow pear tomatoes
1 small handful flat-leaf (Italian) parsley, chopped
60 ml (2 fl oz/1/4 cup) balsamic vinegar
50 g (1 3/4 oz/1/2 cup) grated parmesan cheese

To make the avocado pesto, combine the avocado, garlic, lime juice, herbs, pumpkin seeds, almonds and honey or apple juice in a food processor. Process until smooth. Add 60 ml (2 fl oz/1/4 cup) water and season well with freshly ground black pepper.

Grate the zucchini on a mandolin into spaghetti strips and place into a large bowl. Add the pesto and toss well. Divide among serving bowls. Combine the tomatoes with the parsley and balsamic vinegar, then pile on top of the zucchini. Serve topped with the parmesan cheese.

Lamb burrito with yoghurt mayonnaise

Serves 4

3 garlic cloves, crushed
juice from 1 lemon
1 teaspoon ground cumin
400 g (14 oz) lamb backstrap or loin fillet, fat trimmed and thinly sliced
1 small handful mint, chopped
1 small handful flat-leaf (Italian) parsley, chopped

Yoghurt mayonnaise

125 g (4 1/2 oz/1/2 cup) low-fat plain yoghurt or silken tofu
1/2 teaspoon wholegrain mustard
1 tablespoon chopped coriander (cilantro) leaves
1 garlic clove, crushed

8 large iceberg lettuce leaves
2 large handfuls rocket (arugula)
4 tomatoes, diced

Combine the garlic, lemon juice and cumin in a shallow bowl. Add the lamb and marinate for 15 minutes. Heat a non-stick frying pan over high heat and spray with a little olive oil. Add the lamb and cook over high heat until browned. Transfer the lamb to a bowl and toss with the herbs. Make the yoghurt mayonnaise by combining all the ingredients together. To assemble, fill each lettuce leaf with some of the lamb mixture, some rocket, tomato and 1 tablespoon yoghurt mayonnaise, then roll up to form a parcel. Store any leftover mayonnaise in the refrigerator for up to 1 week.

Spinach and ricotta pie

Serves 4

1 leek, sliced
1 onion, sliced
2 garlic cloves, crushed
500 g (1 lb 2 oz) English spinach or silverbeet (Swiss chard) leaves, shredded
1 large handful rocket (arugula), chopped
40 g (1¹/₂ oz/¹/₄ cup) toasted pine nuts, roughly chopped
1 handful basil, chopped
pinch of ground nutmeg, to taste
500 g (1 lb 2 oz/2 cups) low-fat ricotta cheese or cottage cheese, drained well
8 sheets filo pastry

Preheat the oven to 200°C (400°F/Gas 6). Sauté the leek, onion and garlic with a little water or vegetable stock in a saucepan until soft. Remove from the heat and allow to cool. Wash the spinach or silverbeet well and place in a tea towel (dish towel). Squeeze well to remove any excess moisture. Combine the leek and onion mixture with the leaves, rocket, pine nuts, basil, nutmeg and ricotta. Season with sea salt and ground black pepper.

Line a baking tin with baking paper, then lay 4 sheets of filo in the base of the tin. Spread the filling over the top of the pastry, then top with the remaining 4 filo sheets. Tuck in the edges of the pastry to seal. Spray the top with a little olive oil. Bake for 40–45 minutes, or until golden.

Note Make sure you drain all the excess liquid from the ricotta cheese, otherwise you'll have a soggy crust.

Chicken salad with orange pecan dressing

Serves 2

200 g (7 oz) chicken breast, poached or grilled (broiled)
1 large butter lettuce, torn into pieces
2 tomatoes, sliced
¹/₂ small red onion, sliced

Orange pecan dressing
60 ml (2 fl oz/¹/₄ cup) orange juice
2 oranges, segmented
1 tablespoon honey
1 tablespoon nut oil or linseed oil
1 small handful coriander (cilantro) leaves, chopped
30 g (1 oz/¹/₄ cup) chopped pecans

Shred the chicken. Combine with the lettuce, tomato and onion. Mix the orange pecan dressing ingredients together and pour over the salad just before eating.

Chicken and vegetable soup

Serves 4

1.5 litres (52 fl oz/6 cups) chicken stock
1 tablespoon grated fresh ginger
1 lemon grass stem, finely chopped (white part only)
8 makrut (kaffir lime) leaves, thinly sliced
400 g (14 oz) lean chicken breast, thinly sliced
2 broccoli, cut into florets
1/2 cauliflower, cut into florets
1/4 Savoy cabbage, shredded
250 g (9 oz) shiitake mushrooms
1 handful coriander (cilantro) leaves, chopped

Combine the stock, ginger, lemon grass, makrut leaves and chicken in a large saucepan and bring to the boil. Simmer for 8 minutes, then add the broccoli, cauliflower, cabbage and mushrooms. Cook for a further 10 minutes, or until the vegetables are tender. Fold through the coriander. Ladle the soup into deep bowls and serve.

Note Vegetarians can use vegetable stock and shredded firm tofu in place of the chicken. The chicken can also be replaced with firm white fish, salmon or prawns (shrimp). If using seafood, add it to the saucepan about 5 minutes before serving.

Warm chicken and peach salad with pink grapefruit dressing

Serves 2

2 baby cos (romaine) lettuces, torn into pieces
200 g (7 oz) skinless chicken breasts, grilled (broiled) or roasted and sliced
2 freestone peaches, halved and cut into wedges
1/2 red onion, sliced

Pink grapefruit dressing
2 pink grapefruit
1 small handful mint, chopped
1 tablespoon olive oil or linseed oil

Combine the lettuce, chicken, peaches and onion in a bowl. Make the dressing by peeling the grapefruit and slicing down the side of each segment to free it from its membrane. Squeeze any grapefruit juice from the membrane over a separate bowl. Combine the grapefruit juice with the segments, mint and oil. Pour over the chicken and peach salad and toss well. Divide between serving bowls and serve.

Note Firm poached white fish or cooked and peeled king prawns (shrimp) can be used in place of the chicken. Pineapple or mango can replace the peaches.

The healthy sandwich

When making a healthy sandwich, forget butter and margarine and use heart-healthy spreads and fillings like the ones listed below.

Serves 1

2 slices wholemeal (whole-wheat), rye, spelt or sourdough bread

Fillings

Sliced turkey breast, lettuce, tomato and mashed avocado.

Peeled cooked prawns (shrimp), lettuce, tomato and mashed avocado.

Tinned tuna chunks in spring water (drained), rocket (arugula) and basil pesto.

Poached and sliced chicken breast, mashed avocado, lettuce and sweet chilli sauce.

Grated carrot mixed with a little tahini and lemon juice and topped with lettuce and alfalfa.

Leftover sliced chicken meatloaf (see page 150) or rissoles, lettuce, tomato and sweet chilli sauce.

Grilled (broiled) or barbecued eggplant (aubergine), hummus, English spinach leaves and tomato.

Hard-boiled chopped egg whites, basil pesto, lettuce and tomato.

Curried egg made from 4 hard-boiled egg whites and 1 hard-boiled yolk, curry powder and a spoonful of low-fat mayonnaise topped with lettuce.

Grilled (broiled) or barbecued eggplant (aubergine), dhal (see page 136), zucchini (courgette) and rocket (arugula).

Cold Thai fish cakes (see page 116) with bean sprouts, sweet chilli sauce and lettuce.

Asparagus, smoked salmon or crabmeat and avocado.

Salmon (tinned or smoked) with rocket (arugula) and tomato.

Lean roast pork with home-made spiced apple sauce (see page 142) and butter lettuce.

Lean roast beef with mustard pickle or horseradish, tomato and lettuce.

DINNER

Barbecued fish with sweet chilli and lime

Serves 2

100 ml (3 1/2 fl oz) lime juice
2 garlic cloves, crushed
60 ml (2 fl oz/1/4 cup) sweet chilli sauce
1/2 teaspoon sesame oil
2 x 150 g (5 1/2 oz) pieces firm fish such as swordfish, blue eye cod, tuna steaks
1/4 iceberg lettuce, cut into wedges
1/2 avocado, quartered

Combine the lime juice, garlic, sweet chilli sauce and sesame oil with a pinch of freshly ground black pepper. Place the fish in a shallow bowl and pour over the marinade. Leave to marinate for about 15 minutes.

Cook the fish over a hot barbecue or in a frying pan for a few minutes until cooked through, basting with the marinade during cooking. Transfer to serving plates and accompany with the lettuce wedges and avocado.

Stir-fried garlic and chilli king prawns

Serves 2

1 teaspoon olive oil
300 g (10 1/2 oz) raw king prawns (shrimp), peeled with tails intact
2 garlic cloves, crushed
1 red chilli, sliced (optional)
juice of 1 lime
350 g (12 oz) green vegetables of your choice (good choices are asparagus, bok choy (bok choy) and broccoli)
10 pieces baby corn, halved
100 g (3 1/2 oz/2/3 cup) shiitake mushrooms, sliced
1 tablespoon soy sauce
60 ml (2 fl oz/1/4 cup) mirin

Heat a frying pan over high heat and add the oil. Add the prawns, garlic and chilli, if using, and stir-fry for 1 minute, until the prawns are almost cooked through. Pour over the lime juice and add the green vegetables, corn, mushrooms, soy and mirin. Stir-fry for another 3 minutes, or until the vegetables are cooked but still slightly crisp, adding a little chicken stock or water to the pan if necessary. Serve immediately.

Notes Vegetarians can use firm tofu or tempeh in place of the king prawns (shrimp).

Mirin, a Japanese sweet rice wine, is available from most supermarkets and Asian food stores. You can also use sake or Chinese rice wine.

Crab omelette

Serves 1

1 egg
4 egg whites
1 handful baby English spinach leaves
60 g (2^{1}/$_{4}$ oz) cooked crabmeat
1 spring onion (scallion), sliced
1 tablespoon oyster sauce, to drizzle

Beat the egg and egg whites together. Pour into a hot non-stick frying pan lightly sprayed with olive oil and set over medium heat. Stir the egg mixture with a fork, moving the cooked egg at the edge of the pan into the centre as it sets.

Add the spinach, crabmeat, spring onion and a little freshly ground black pepper. Leave over the heat for a few seconds to further set the base. Tip out onto a serving plate and fold in half. Spoon over the oyster sauce and serve.

Roast vegetables with grilled feta

Serves 2

1 red capsicum (pepper), cut into chunks
1 yellow capsicum (pepper), cut into chunks
1 red onion, cut into chunks
2 zucchini (courgettes), cut into chunks
1 eggplant (aubergine), cut into chunks
2 garlic cloves, crushed
100 g (3^{1}/$_{2}$ oz) low-fat feta or ricotta cheese, crumbled
2 tablespoons chopped flat-leaf (Italian) parsley

Preheat the oven to 220°C (425°F/Gas 7). Scatter the capsicum, red onion, zucchini, eggplant and garlic over a baking tray lined with baking paper and spray with a little olive oil. Roast for 25–30 minutes, or until the vegetables are tender and golden.

Top the vegetables with the feta or ricotta and transfer the tray to a hot grill (broiler). Cook for 2 minutes to brown the cheese. Sprinkle with the parsley and serve.

Marinated lamb cutlets with cherry tomato and feta salad

Serves 2

juice from 1 lemon
1 teaspoon lemon zest
2 teaspoons chopped oregano
2 garlic cloves, crushed
300 g (10^1/$_2$ oz) lean double lamb cutlets
125 g (4^1/$_2$ oz) cherry tomatoes, halved
125 g (4^1/$_2$ oz) yellow pear tomatoes, halved
1 tablespoon chopped flat-leaf (Italian) parsley
40 g (1^1/$_2$ oz/^{1}/$_4$ cup) crumbled low-fat feta cheese

Combine the lemon juice, zest, oregano and garlic in a shallow bowl. Add the lamb and marinate for 10 minutes, then remove from the marinade. Cook in a hot frying pan for 3–4 minutes on each side.

Combine the tomato, parsley and feta. Divide between two serving plates, add the cooked lamb and serve.

Zucchini pancakes

Serves 4

500 g (1 lb 2 oz) grated zucchini (courgette)
2 spring onions (scallions), sliced
1 handful chopped coriander (cilantro) leaves
3 eggs
60 g (2 oz/^{1}/$_2$ cup) soy flour

Squeeze out the moisture from the zucchini. Place the zucchini into a mixing bowl with the spring onion, coriander, eggs and flour. Add pepper to taste. Mix well.

Place the batter, spreading 2 tablespoons for each pancake, into a lightly oiled non-stick pan. Cook over medium heat for about 3 minutes each side until golden and crisp.

Serve alone or with shiitake mushrooms, tofu, oyster sauce and chopped chilli.

Veal saltimbocca with rocket and parmesan salad

Serves 2

4 lean slices prosciutto
4 x 60 g (2¼ oz) pieces thinly sliced veal steaks
12 sage leaves
1 teaspoon olive oil
1 garlic clove, crushed
125 ml (4 fl oz/½ cup) sweet marsala wine
2 large handfuls rocket (arugula)
2 tablespoons shaved parmesan cheese

Press 1 slice of prosciutto onto each piece of veal and top with 3 sage leaves. Heat a large non-stick frying pan with the olive oil over high heat. Add the veal steaks, sage side down, and cook for 1 minute until the base is crisp and golden. Season with a little freshly ground black pepper and the garlic, then turn over and cook the other side for 1 minute. Add the marsala to the pan and cook for a few seconds until the liquid is slightly thickened.

Arrange on serving plates next to the combined rocket and parmesan cheese. Pour over any remaining sauce.

Vegetable curry

Serves 4

3 tablespoons red curry paste
1 onion, finely diced
1 litre (35 fl oz/4 cups) vegetable stock
60 ml (2 fl oz/¼ cup) light coconut milk
1 eggplant (aubergine), cut into chunks
4 zucchini (courgettes), cut into chunks
300 g (10½ oz) pumpkin, cut into chunks
400 g (14 oz) tin chickpeas, drained
1 small handful coriander (cilantro) leaves, chopped

Mix the curry paste and onion together in a saucepan, then cook for about 30 seconds over medium heat. Add the stock, coconut milk, eggplant, zucchini, pumpkin and chickpeas. Cover and simmer for 10 minutes until the vegetables are tender. Thicken if necessary with a little cornflour (cornstarch). Fold through the coriander just before serving.

The lean shepherd's pie

Serves 6

1 quantity bolognaise sauce (see page 109)
800 g (1 lb 12 oz) Jap (Kent) pumpkin, cut into chunks
    and steamed
30 g (1 oz/$1/4$ cup) grated low-fat cheese
pinch of ground nutmeg

Preheat the oven to 200°C (400°F/Gas 6). Spoon the bolognaise sauce into six individual dishes or one large baking dish and set aside. Place the pumpkin chunks over the top of the bolognaise sauce, then sprinkle with the cheese and nutmeg. Bake for 30–40 minutes, or until the pie is hot throughout and golden on top.

Ocean trout with rocket and tomato salad

Serves 2

2 x 150 g (5$1/2$ oz) ocean trout fillets
1 teaspoon olive oil
2 large handfuls rocket (arugula)
125 g (4$1/2$ oz) cherry tomatoes, halved
30 g (1 oz/$1/4$ cup) shaved parmesan cheese
balsamic vinegar, to drizzle

Season the trout with freshly ground black pepper. Heat the oil in a frying pan over medium-high heat. Cook the fillets for a few minutes each side until just cooked through. Toss the rocket with the tomato, then divide between two plates. Transfer the trout to the plates and garnish the salad with the parmesan cheese and a drizzle of balsamic vinegar.

Roast chicken salad with hazelnut dressing

Serves 2

4 large handfuls assorted leafy salad greens, such as baby English spinach leaves, rocket (arugula) and butter lettuce
200 g (7 oz) roast chicken breast, skin removed and shredded (see Note)
1 firm pear, cut into slices
1/2 red onion, sliced

Hazelnut dressing
1 tablespoon hazelnut oil or cold-pressed olive oil
2 tablespoons lemon juice
2 tablespoons orange juice
1 teaspoon orange zest
1 tablespoon finely chopped chervil or parsley
1 tablespoon chopped toasted hazelnuts

To make the hazelnut dressing, combine all the dressing ingredients in a small bowl, then set aside.

Combine the salad leaves, chicken and finely sliced pear, then pour over the dressing and mix well. Divide between serving bowls and serve.

Note A home-made or store-bought roast chicken is fine to have occasionally, but remove the skin before eating.

Veal cutlets with sautéed spinach

Serves 2

2 lean veal cutlets, trimmed of fat
2 garlic cloves, crushed
250 g (9 oz) English spinach leaves, washed and dried
squeeze of lemon juice
1 teaspoon seeded mustard

Preheat the oven to 220°C (425°F/Gas 7). Spray an ovenproof frying pan with a little olive oil and heat over high heat. Sear the veal cutlets on both sides until browned. Place the pan and veal in the hot oven for another 5 minutes to finish cooking.

Meanwhile, in a separate frying pan, stir-fry the garlic, spinach and lemon juice for 1 minute until the leaves are wilted. Season with some freshly ground black pepper. Divide the spinach between serving plates and top with the veal. Spread a little mustard over the veal and serve.

Dhal with green beans and almonds

Serves 4

Dhal

250 g (9 oz/1 cup) red lentils
1 litre (35 fl oz/4 cups) vegetable stock
1 onion, finely diced
1 teaspoon grated fresh ginger
2 garlic cloves, crushed
4 tomatoes, peeled and chopped (see Note)
2 carrots, finely grated
1/2 teaspoon ground turmeric
2 teaspoons garam marsala

500 g (1 lb 2 oz) green beans
40 g (1 1/2 oz/1/4 cup) sun-dried tomatoes, drained
  and thinly sliced
2 tablespoons lemon juice
1 small handful parsley, chopped
25 g (1 oz/1/4 cup) flaked almonds, toasted

To make the dhal, combine the lentils, stock, onion, ginger, garlic, tomato, carrot, turmeric and garam marsala in a saucepan. Simmer gently for 30 minutes, or until the lentils are tender. Add more stock or water if necessary.

Steam the beans until tender. Transfer to a bowl and toss with the sundried tomato, lemon juice, parsley and almonds, then season with freshly ground black pepper. Arrange the beans on plates and spoon over the dhal.

Note To peel tomatoes, score a cross in the base of the tomato and plunge into boiling water for 30 seconds. Put into a bowl of iced water and peel the skin away.

Stir-fried chicken and snow peas

Serves 2

2 skinless chicken breasts, thinly sliced
2 garlic cloves, crushed
1 teaspoon chopped fresh ginger
2 large handfuls snow peas (mangetout), topped and
  tailed
2 tablespoons soy sauce
60 ml (2 fl oz/1/4 cup) mirin
cashew nuts and sliced spring onion (scallions), to
  garnish (optional)

Sauté the chicken in a hot non-stick frying pan or wok until cooked through and browned, adding a touch of water every now and then while cooking. Add the garlic, ginger, snow peas, soy sauce and mirin, and toss through until combined and the snow peas are warmed through, but still crisp. Spoon into serving bowls and garnish with the cashew nuts and spring onions.

Warm tuna and bean tabouleh

Serves 4

4 x 120 g (4^1/$_4$ oz) tuna steaks
2 garlic cloves, crushed
juice from 1 lemon
1/2 teaspoon ground cumin

Bean tabouleh

1 large handful parsley, chopped
1 handful mint, chopped
60 g (2 oz/2 cups) English spinach leaves, chopped
3 tomatoes, diced
400 g (14 oz) tin cannellini beans, drained
2 spring onions (scallions), sliced
2 garlic cloves, crushed
30 g (1 oz/^{1}/$_4$ cup) chopped walnuts
150 g (5^1/$_2$ oz/1 cup) crumbled low-fat feta cheese
1 teaspoon ground cumin
juice of 1 lemon
1 tablespoon cold-pressed olive oil or linseed oil

Combine the tuna with the garlic, lemon juice and cumin. Marinate while you prepare the bean tabouleh.

To make the bean tabouleh, combine all the ingredients in a bowl and mix well. Heat a frying pan until hot and spray lightly with a little oil. Add the tuna and cook for about 3 minutes on each side, or until cooked to your liking. Divide the tabouleh among serving bowls and top with the tuna steaks.

Note You can also use sliced and grilled (broiled) lamb backstrap instead of the tuna.

Mushroom soup with fish, lime, chilli and coriander

Serves 4

1.5 litres (52 fl oz/6 cups) chicken stock
1 lemon grass stem, finely chopped (white part only)
300 g (10^1/$_2$ oz) assorted mushrooms, quartered
500 g (1 lb 2 oz) firm fish fillet, cut into chunks
2 spring onions (scallions), sliced
2 tablespoons fish sauce
1 handful coriander (cilantro) leaves
juice of 1/2 lime
4 handfuls baby English spinach leaves

Put the stock, lemon grass and mushrooms in a large saucepan and simmer over low heat for 5–10 minutes. Add the fish chunks, spring onion and fish sauce, then simmer for a further 2 minutes until the fish is just cooked. Fold in the coriander and drizzle in the lime juice. Divide the spinach leaves between large serving bowls and pour over the soup. Serve immediately.

Note Silken tofu or skinless chicken breast can be used in place of the fish.

Pork and vegetable san choi bao

Serves 4

2 garlic cloves, crushed
1 onion, diced
1 teaspoon sesame oil
400 g (14 oz) minced (ground) lean pork
150 g (5¹/2 oz) shiitake mushrooms, sliced
2 tablespoons soy sauce
60 ml (2 fl oz/¹/4 cup) mirin or dry sherry
150 g (5¹/2 oz) snow peas (mangetout), sliced
1 large handful bean sprouts
2 spring onions (scallions), sliced
juice from 2 limes
1 teaspoon honey
165 g (5³/4 oz/1 cup) chopped fresh pineapple
1 handful Vietnamese mint or coriander (cilantro)
   leaves, chopped
iceberg lettuce leaves, to serve

Put the garlic, onion and oil into a hot frying pan and sauté until golden. Add the pork and mushrooms and continue cooking for 5 minutes, or until browned. Add the soy sauce, mirin or dry sherry, snow peas, bean sprouts, spring onion, lime juice and honey. Cook for 2 minutes, then add the pineapple and herbs and stir together.

Pile the pork stir-fry onto a large serving plate, with the lettuce leaves alongside. To eat, spoon the stir-fry into the lettuce cups and roll them up. Serve with a dipping sauce of sweet chilli sauce, if you like.

Note I like to mince my own pork to ensure it's lean. Your butcher can do the same thing for you on request.

Coq au vin

Serves 4

400 g (14 oz) skinless chicken breast
60 g (2¹/4 oz) lean bacon, sliced
2 garlic cloves, crushed
1 onion, diced
250 ml (9 fl oz/1 cup) red wine
1 litre (35 fl oz/4 cups) chicken stock
3 carrots, chopped
500 g (1 lb 2 oz) mushrooms, quartered
300 g (10¹/2 oz) green beans, trimmed
2 red capsicums (peppers), diced
1 tablespoon thyme

Combine the chicken, bacon, garlic and onion in a large saucepan and brown, using a little water to stop the mixture from sticking. Pour in the red wine and chicken stock, then add the carrot and mushrooms. Cover and simmer for about 30 minutes.

Add the beans, capsicum and thyme and simmer for a further 10 minutes. Thicken the sauce with a little cornflour (cornstarch) if necessary and season with freshly ground black pepper. Spoon into serving bowls.

Spicy braised fish with shiitake mushrooms

Serves 4

1 litre (35 fl oz/4 cups) chicken or vegetable stock
60 ml (2 fl oz/¼ cup) oyster sauce
2 star anise
4 cm (1½ inch) piece cassia bark
200 g (7 oz) shiitake mushrooms
1 garlic clove, chopped
1 tablespoon grated fresh ginger
1 tablespoon fish sauce
4 x 185 g (6½ oz) firm white fish fillets, such as blue eye cod
2 handfuls snow peas (mangetout), trimmed, or bok choy (pak choy)

Combine the stock, oyster sauce, star anise, cassia bark, mushrooms, garlic, ginger and fish sauce in a wide, deep saucepan. Cover and simmer for about 10 minutes over medium heat, or until the flavours have infused into the stock. Add the fish and simmer for a further 6–8 minutes, or until the fish is cooked through (the fish should flake easily). Add the snow peas or bok choy and cook for a further 1 minute.

Place the fish into shallow serving bowls and ladle over the stock, shiitake mushrooms and greens. Serve hot.

Note For a vegetarian meal, replace the fish with 750 g (1 lb 10 oz) silken tofu.

My best smoked salmon caesar salad

Serves 2

2 baby cos (romaine) lettuces, leaves washed and separated
200 g (7 oz) sliced smoked salmon
40 g (1¼ oz) lean prosciutto or bacon, cooked until crisp
125 g (4½ oz) cherry tomatoes, halved
2 eggs, soft-poached or soft-boiled
2 tablespoons shaved or shredded parmesan cheese
1 tablespoon chopped flat-leaf (Italian) parsley

Caesar dressing

1 garlic clove, crushed
2 anchovy fillets, mashed with a fork
1 tablespoon lemon juice or white wine vinegar
½ teaspoon dijon mustard
1 teaspoon honey
200 g (7 oz/heaped ¾ cup) low-fat plain yoghurt or silken tofu

First, make the dressing. Combine all the ingredients in a bowl, season with freshly ground black pepper and mix well. Set aside.

Arrange the cos lettuce leaves in two large serving bowls. Top with the salmon, bacon and cherry tomato. Place an egg on the top, then garnish with parmesan cheese and parsley. Serve with 2–3 tablespoons of the dressing.

Asparagus salad with roasted salmon fillets

Serves 2

2 x 150 g (5 1/2 oz) salmon fillets
1 teaspoon wholegrain mustard
juice from 1/2 lemon
350 g (12 oz/2 bunches) asparagus, trimmed
juice from 1/2 orange
1 large handful rocket (arugula)
50 g (1 3/4 oz/1/3 cup) crumbled low-fat feta cheese
1 tablespoon chopped walnuts

Dressing
1 teaspoon chopped oregano
1 garlic clove, crushed
juice from 1/2 lemon
1 teaspoon honey

Preheat the oven to 200°C (400°F/Gas 6). First make the dressing. Combine all the ingredients, and season to taste with a little freshly ground black pepper. Set aside until needed.

Season the salmon with a smear of mustard and a drizzle of lemon juice. Roast in the oven for about 10 minutes, or until the fillets are just cooked through. Meanwhile, cook the asparagus in a hot, lightly oiled chargrill pan or non-stick frying pan for 2–3 minutes. Drizzle over a little orange juice halfway through cooking.

Arrange the rocket on a serving plate. Place the asparagus on top and scatter over the feta and walnuts. Top with the salmon and drizzle over the dressing.

Pork cutlets with spiced apple and Savoy cabbage

Serves 2

Spiced apple sauce
2 apples, peeled and thinly sliced
1/2 teaspoon ground cinnamon
pinch of ground cloves
2 teaspoons honey
1 tablespoon lemon juice

2 lean pork cutlets
200 g (7 oz/2 2/3 cups) very thinly sliced savoy cabbage
60 ml (2 fl oz/1/4 cup) chicken stock
1 tablespoon chopped chives

Put the apple, cinnamon, cloves, honey and lemon juice in a saucepan and cook over medium heat for 5 minutes, or until the apples are soft. Remove from the heat and set aside. Cook the pork cutlets for 3 minutes each side in a hot frying pan greased with 1 teaspoon olive oil.

Stir-fry the cabbage with the chicken stock in another hot pan or wok until the cabbage is just wilted. Fold through the chives. Divide the cabbage between serving plates and top with the pork and spiced apple.

Whole barbecued snapper

Serves 6

800 g (1 lb 12 oz) snapper, scaled, cleaned and gutted
1 lemon grass stem, finely chopped (white part only)
2 tablespoons grated fresh ginger
60 ml (2 fl oz/1/4 cup) mirin or dry sherry
2 teaspoons soft brown sugar or grated palm sugar
2 tablespoons soy sauce
2 spring onions (scallions), sliced
1 handful Vietnamese mint or coriander (cilantro)
  leaves, chopped
Asian-style coleslaw, to serve (see Note)

Preheat your barbecue to hot. Wash the fish and pat dry
with paper towels. Cut three slits down both sides of the
fish. Place the fish in the centre of a large piece of foil
(shiny side up). Combine the lemon grass, ginger, mirin
or sherry, sugar and soy sauce. Rub the mixture over both
sides and inside the fish, then pour the rest over the top.
Sprinkle over half the spring onion and herbs, then seal
the fish well in the foil, ensuring there are no gaps.

Place onto the hot barbecue grill plate and cook for about
10 minutes each side, or until cooked through (the flesh
should be white to the bone). Garnish with the remaining
spring onion and herbs, and serve with the coleslaw.

Note To make the coleslaw, mix 300 g (10 1/2 oz/4 cups)
sliced Savoy cabbage with 2 grated carrots, 2 spring onions
(scallions), 1 handful chopped Vietnamese mint or coriander
(cilantro) leaves and 1 handful chopped mint. Toss with
125 ml (4 fl oz/1/2 cup) lime juice, 4 tablespoons fish sauce
and 3 teaspoons soft brown sugar or grated palm sugar.

Lean chilli con carne

Serves 2

250 g (9 oz) minced (ground) lean beef or veal
1 onion, finely diced
2 garlic cloves, crushed
1 red chilli, seeded and sliced
1 teaspoon ground cumin
1 carrot, grated
1 stick celery, sliced
250 ml (9 fl oz/1 cup) beef stock
2 tablespoons tomato paste (concentrated purée)
  with no added salt
1 teaspoon sugar
2 tomatoes, peeled and chopped (see Note)
200 g (7 oz) red kidney beans, drained
2 teaspoons chopped flat-leaf (Italian) parsley

Sauté the mince in a hot pan until brown, without using
any added fat. Pour over 500 ml (17 fl oz/2 cups) of
boiling water, then boil for 1 minute. Drain the mince in a
colander to remove the extra saturated fat and return the
mince to the pan.

Add the onion, garlic, chilli, cumin, carrot, celery and
stock. Cover, reduce the heat and simmer for 15 minutes.
Remove the lid, add the tomato paste, sugar, chopped
tomato and beans, and pepper to taste. Cook for another
5 minutes until thick and rich, adding a little more stock if
needed. Serve in bowls and top with parsley.

Note To peel tomatoes, make a tiny slit at the top end of the
tomato and plunge into boiling water for 30 seconds.
Transfer to a bowl of iced water , then peel off the skin.

Egyptian lamb salad

Serves 4

2 teaspoons ground cumin
1 teaspoon ground cinnamon
4 garlic cloves, crushed
2 teaspoons honey
1 teaspoon freshly ground black pepper
juice from 2 lemons
400 g (14 oz) lamb backstrap or loin fillet, thinly sliced

Salad
4 Lebanese (short) cucumbers, halved and sliced
1 carrot, thinly sliced or shredded
1 spring onion (scallion), sliced
1 handful walnuts
4 handfuls rocket (arugula)
4 dates, sliced
100 g (3 1/2 oz/2/3 cup) crumbled low-fat feta cheese
juice from 1 lemon
2 teaspoons honey
1 tablespoon linseed oil or cold-pressed olive oil

Combine the cumin, cinnamon, garlic, honey, pepper and lemon juice in a shallow bowl. Add the lamb and allow to marinate while you prepare the salad. Combine the salad ingredients in a bowl, except for the lemon juice, honey and oil. Remove the lamb from the marinade and stir-fry over high heat in a frying pan until golden. Toss the lamb with the salad, along with the lemon juice, honey and oil.

Note Vegetarians can use 400 g (14 oz) tinned drained chickpeas instead of the lamb.

Vegetable tagine

Serves 4

2 garlic cloves, chopped
1 red onion, cut into wedges
1 leek, sliced
2 teaspoons ground cumin
1 teaspoon ground ginger
1/2 teaspoon ground cinnamon
1/2 teaspoon cayenne pepper
1/2 teaspoon ground turmeric
500 ml (17 fl oz/2 cups) vegetable stock
400 g (14 oz) tin tomato juice
400 g (14 oz) butternut pumpkin (squash), cut into chunks
400 g (14 oz) tin chickpeas, rinsed and drained
2 zucchini (courgettes), chopped
1 red capsicum (pepper), diced
90 g (3 1/4 oz/1 bunch) coriander (cilantro), chopped

Sauté the garlic, onion and leek with a little water or stock until soft. Add the cumin, ginger, cinnamon, cayenne pepper and turmeric and cook for 30 seconds. Add the stock, tomato juice and pumpkin. Cook over medium heat for 10–15 minutes, or until the pumpkin is just tender. Add the chickpeas, zucchini and capsicum and cook for a further 2 minutes until warmed through. Fold through the coriander and serve.

Satay vegetable kebabs

Serves 4

8–10 skewers (see Note)
300 g (10 1/2 oz) firm tofu or chicken breast, cubed
2 zucchini (courgettes), cut into chunks
250 g (9 oz) cherry tomatoes
300 g (10 1/2 oz) button mushrooms
1 red capsicum (pepper), cut into chunks
1/2 pineapple, cut into chunks
salad leaves, to serve

Satay sauce
1/2 onion, chopped
2 garlic cloves, chopped
1 teaspoon chopped fresh ginger
60 g (2 1/4 oz/1/4 cup) crunchy peanut butter
2 tablespoons soy sauce
1 tablespoon maple syrup or honey
squeeze of lime juice

Preheat the grill (broiler) to hot. Thread the tofu or chicken, zucchini, tomatoes, mushrooms, capsicum and pineapple chunks onto skewers. Arrange onto a tray lined with foil and spray with a little olive oil. Grill (broil) for 10–15 minutes, or until golden. Make sure to turn the kebabs over halfway through cooking.

Meanwhile, make the satay sauce by combining the onion, garlic and ginger in a food processor. Process until combined, then spoon into a saucepan and cook over medium heat for 3 minutes, using a little water if necessary to stop it sticking. Add the peanut butter, soy sauce, maple syrup or honey, lime juice and 60 ml (2 fl oz/1/4 cup) water. Cook for another minute, adding more water if necessary. Arrange the kebabs over a bed of salad leaves and spoon over the satay sauce. Serve immediately.

Note If using wooden skewers, soak them in cold water for 15 minutes before using.

Warm tuna with steamed beans, rocket and tomato

Serves 2

2 x 185 g (6¹/2 oz) tuna steaks
10 cherry tomatoes
2 large handfuls green beans
¹/4 red onion, sliced
50 g (1³/4 oz/¹/3 cup) low-fat feta cheese, crumbled
1 tablespoon chopped walnuts
1 tablespoon chopped flat-leaf (Italian) parsley
2 large handfuls rocket (arugula)
balsamic vinegar, to serve

Season one side of each tuna steak with a little freshly ground black pepper. Heat a little olive oil on a hot char-grill pan. Add the tuna steaks and cook for about 3 minutes each side, or until cooked through.

Meanwhile, add the tomatoes to the pan to heat through. Lightly steam the green beans for 3–5 minutes. Place the beans into a bowl along with the warmed cherry tomatoes, onion, feta, walnuts, parsley and rocket. Toss together well and divide between serving plates. Arrange the chargrilled tuna over the top, then drizzle with a little balsamic vinegar and serve.

Warm beef salad

Serves 2

300 g (10¹/2 oz) lean rump steak
2 Lebanese (short) cucumbers, sliced
1 red capsicum (pepper), sliced
¹/2 red onion, sliced
2 tomatoes, cut into wedges
2 large handfuls bean sprouts
1 handful Vietnamese mint or coriander (cilantro)
   leaves, chopped
1 handful mint, chopped

Dressing
juice from 2 limes
2 tablespoons fish sauce
3 tablespoons sweet chilli sauce
2 garlic cloves, crushed

Season the steaks with some freshly ground black pepper. Cook the steaks in a very hot frying pan until medium-rare (a couple minutes each side, depending on the thickness of the steaks). Remove the steaks from the heat and allow to rest for 5–10 minutes.

Combine the cucumber, capsicum, onion, tomato, bean shoots and herbs in a serving bowl. Slice the steak into thin strips and add to the salad. Mix the dressing ingredients together, toss through the salad and serve.

Chicken meatloaf

Serves 6–8

500 g (1 lb 2 oz) minced (ground) skinless chicken
   breast
2 egg whites, lightly beaten
1 spring onion (scallion), thinly sliced
1 carrot, grated
1 red capsicum (pepper), finely diced
100 g (3^1/2 oz/^{2}/3 cup) shiitake mushrooms, finely
chopped
1 teaspoon grated fresh ginger
1 garlic clove, crushed
1 small handful coriander (cilantro) leaves, chopped
25 g (1 oz/1 bunch) chives, chopped
1 tablespoon soy sauce
steamed green vegetables, to serve

Preheat the oven to 170°C (325°F/Gas 3). Combine the
chicken and the egg whites in a large bowl and mix
together well. Add the spring onion, carrot, capsicum,
mushrooms, ginger, garlic, herbs and soy sauce. Mix
together until combined. Pack the chicken mixture into a
medium-sized loaf tin lined with baking paper.

Bake the meatloaf for 50–60 minutes, or until firm to the
touch. Remove the meatloaf from the oven and allow to
stand for 10 minutes before removing from the tin. Cut
into slices and serve with steamed green vegetables.

Note If you like, serve the meatloaf with a store-bought
tomato chutney on the side.

Oven-baked fish fillet

Serves 2

2 x 200 g (7 oz) firm fish fillets, such as blue eye cod,
   snapper or salmon
2 teaspoons grated fresh ginger
^{1}/4 teapoon sesame oil
2 teaspoons chopped coriander (cilantro) leaves
   or chives
1 lime, thinly sliced, plus extra, to garnish (optional)
iceberg lettuce leaves, to serve
1 teaspoon sesame seeds, toasted, to serve

Preheat the oven to 200°C (400°F/Gas 6). Put two sheets
of baking paper or foil, large enough to enclose the fish,
onto a work surface. Arrange the fish in the centre of the
paper or foil. Sprinkle the fish with the ginger, sesame oil,
herbs and some freshly ground black pepper. Lay the
lime slices over the top.

Completely enclose the fish in the paper or foil. If using
paper, it's a good idea to use clips or wooden pegs to
stop the paper from opening while cooking. Bake for
about 15 minutes, or until the parcels are puffed out and
the fish has cooked through. Transfer the parcels to
serving plates and serve with the lettuce and sesame
seeds. Open the parcels just before eating and serve
with a little soy sauce on the side. Garnish with lime
wedges if you like.

Spicy laksa

Serves 2

1 leek, sliced
2–3 tablespoons laksa paste
750 ml (26 fl oz/3 cups) vegetable or chicken stock
60 ml (2 fl oz/1/4 cup) light coconut milk
200 g (7 oz) chicken breast, thinly sliced
1 red capsicum (pepper), sliced
50 g (13/4 oz) baby corn
50 g (13/4 oz) snow peas (mangetout)
juice from 1/2 lime
1 handful coriander (cilantro) leaves, chopped
100 g (31/2 oz) bean sprouts

Heat a deep saucepan over high heat. Add the leek and a little water and stir-fry for 2 minutes until softened. Add the laksa paste and cook, stirring, for 1 minute. Add the stock and coconut milk and bring to the boil, then reduce the heat to a simmer. Add the chicken, capsicum and corn and simmer for 5 minutes, or until the meat is cooked. Add the snow peas, lime juice and coriander just before serving. Divide the bean sprouts between serving bowls. Ladle in the hot soup and serve immediately.

Note The chicken can be replaced with the same quantity of firm white fish fillets or salmon, cut into chunks. Vegetarians can use vegetable stock and silken tofu in place of the chicken; just slice and place over the bean sprouts in the serving bowls, then pour in the hot soup.

Moussaka

Serves 6

2 eggplants (aubergines), peeled and thinly sliced
1 quantity bolognaise sauce (see page 109)
40 g (11/2 oz/1/2 cup) grated parmesan cheese

White sauce
1 leek, chopped
500 g (1 lb 2 oz) low-fat ricotta cheese
125 ml (4 fl oz/1/2 cup) vegetable or chicken stock
pinch of ground nutmeg, to taste

First make the white sauce. Sauté the leek in a little water in a frying pan until soft. Tip into a food processor along with the ricotta cheese. Process until smooth and creamy. Add a little stock — just enough to make the sauce smooth and spreadable. Season to taste with a little freshly ground black pepper and a pinch of nutmeg.

Preheat the oven to 180°C (350°F/Gas 4). Place the eggplant slices under a hot grill (broiler) and cook until lightly golden on both sides (alternatively, you can cook in a chargrill pan using no oil). Arrange half the eggplant slices over the base of a 25 cm (10 inch) baking dish. Pour over the bolognaise sauce, then arrange the remaining eggplant slices over the top. Spread the white sauce over the eggplant and sprinkle with the parmesan cheese. Bake for 45 minutes, or until heated through.

Note You can also use the vegetarian bolognaise sauce (see page 109), and silken tofu in the white sauce instead of the ricotta — just don't add the stock, if doing so.

Chilli mussels

Serves 2

1 onion, finely diced
3 garlic cloves, crushed
1 teaspoon olive oil
400 g (14 oz) tin crushed tomatoes, or peeled and
    chopped fresh tomatoes
1/2 teaspoon hot smoked paprika
1 red chilli, sliced
125 ml (4 fl oz/1/2 cup) chicken stock
1 kg (2 lb 4 oz) cleaned mussels in their shells
1 small handful flat-leaf (Italian) parsley, chopped

Sauté the onion and garlic in the olive oil in a large
saucepan for 1 minute. Add the tomato, paprika, chilli
and stock. Cover and simmer for 10 minutes. Add the
mussels, stir through, cover and cook for a further
5 minutes until they've all opened. Discard any that don't
open. Stir through the parsley and serve immediately in
large bowls.

Note Mussels must be bought alive, as any that are dead
may be toxic. The shells should be uncracked and
closed, or should close when tapped on the bench.
Discard any that don't close.

Turbo red chicken curry

Serves 2

250 g (9 oz) skinless chicken breasts, cut into chunks
1 onion, sliced
2 heaped tablespoons red curry paste
500 ml (17 fl oz/2 cups) chicken stock
1 red capsicum (pepper), sliced
150 g (51/2 oz) mushrooms, sliced
150 g (51/2 oz) baby corn, halved
60 ml (2 fl oz/1/4 cup) low-fat milk
1 small handful coriander (cilantro) leaves, chopped

Sauté the chicken and onion in a saucepan until golden
using a little water to stop them sticking. Add the curry
paste, stock, capsicum, mushroom, baby corn and milk.
Cook over medium heat for 3 minutes. Thicken with a little
cornflour (cornstarch) if necessary. Serve in bowls,
garnished with the coriander.

Notes You can replace the chicken with lean pork,
prawns (shrimp), firm white fish or tofu and add with the
stock and vegetables, rather than at the start of cooking.

Make sure to first mix the cornflour with a little water when
thickening the curry.

Thai prawn salad

Serves 2

2 oranges, peeled and segmented
2 pink grapefruit, peeled and segmented
75 g (2¹/₂ oz/1 cup) bean sprouts, trimmed
1 handful bean shoots
1 small red papaya, peeled, seeded and cut into
   chunks
1 handful Vietnamese mint or coriander (cilantro)
   leaves, chopped
1 handful mint, chopped
¹/₂ red onion, sliced
2 spring onions (scallions), sliced
¹/₂ yellow capsicum (pepper), sliced
12 raw prawns (shrimp), peeled with tails intact
1 tablespoon chopped roasted cashew nuts, to garnish

Dressing
60 ml (2 fl oz/¹/₄ cup) lime juice
1 teaspoon honey
2 tablespoons fish sauce
1 garlic clove, crushed

Combine the citrus segments, bean sprouts and shoots, papaya, herbs, red onion, spring onion and capsicum in a bowl. Mix the dressing ingredients together and set aside. Stir-fry the prawns in a hot pan with a little olive oil for 1–2 minutes, or until cooked and golden. Season with freshly ground black pepper.

Add the prawns and dressing to the salad and toss well. Divide between serving plates and garnish with the cashew nuts. Serve immediately.

Chicken and prawn salad with lime dressing

Serves 4

Lime dressing
125 ml (4 fl oz/¹/₂ cup) lime juice
2 garlic cloves, crushed
80 ml (2¹/₂ fl oz/¹/₃ cup) fish sauce
1 red chilli, chopped
1 tablespoon honey or grated palm sugar

¹/₂ iceberg lettuce, finely shredded
2 large carrots, grated
1 red capsicum (pepper), thinly sliced
1 handful Vietnamese mint or coriander (cilantro)
   leaves, chopped
1 handful mint, chopped
400 g (14 oz) skinless chicken breast, steamed or
   poached
400 g (14 oz) cooked and peeled king prawns
   (shrimp)
1 avocado, diced

First make the lime dressing. Combine all the ingredients in a small bowl and set aside. Mix the lettuce, carrot, capsicum, herbs, chicken and prawns in a large bowl. Pour over the dressing and gently mix together. Pile into serving dishes and garnish with the diced avocado.

Note You can also use a store-bought barbecue chicken (with skin removed) instead of the poached chicken and prawns. Firm white fish fillets and lean grilled (broiled) pork also combine well in this dish.

Roast marinated pork with bok choy

Serves 4

60 ml (2 fl oz/¼ cup) sweet soy sauce
4 garlic cloves, crushed
1 teaspoon grated fresh ginger
60 ml (2 fl oz/¼ cup) mirin
2 teaspoons soft brown sugar

500 g (1 lb 2 oz) lean pork tenderloin
4 bok choy (pak choy)
60 ml (2 fl oz/¼ cup) chicken stock
¼ teaspoon sesame oil

Combine the soy sauce, half the garlic, the ginger, mirin and brown sugar in a shallow bowl. Add the pork and allow to marinate for at least 4 hours or overnight in the refrigerator.

Preheat the oven to 200°C (400°F/Gas 6). Half-fill a roasting tin with water. Remove the pork from the marinade, reserving the marinade, and place on a wire rack that sits over the roasting tin. Transfer the pork and roasting tin to the oven and cook for 25–30 minutes, basting with the reserved marinade throughout. Remove the pork and allow to rest for 5 minutes before slicing.

While the pork is resting, stir-fry the bok choy in a hot wok with the remaining garlic, the stock and sesame oil. Serve with the sliced pork.

Note Sweet soy sauce (kecap manis) is available in the Asian section in your supermarket or in Asian food stores. Mirin is a sweet rice wine available in supermarkets and Asian food stores.

DESSERTS AND SWEET TREATS

These desserts and sweet treats fall into the 20 per cent part of the 80/20 diet. I'm the first to admit that I really have a sweet tooth. But if you follow the 80/20 principle, you can have sweet foods occasionally and still maintain your healthy eating plan and weight-loss goal. The following sweets and cakes are not included in your meal plan. They have been designed to curb your sweet cravings once in a while. As with all the recipes, you'll find lots of choices that not only make quick and simple treats, but are also great for healthy entertaining. If you really need a sweet fix after dinner, then stick to seasonal fresh fruit and save these yummy treats for once or twice a week.

Chilled berry compote

Serves 6

500 g (1 lb 2 oz) mixed frozen berries
310 ml (10³/4 fl oz/1¹/4 cups) apple or grape juice
500 g (1 lb 2 oz/2 cups) low-fat plain yoghurt, to serve

Put the berries in a food processor. Add the apple or grape juice and process until smooth. Pour the compote into serving dishes and swirl in a scoop of yoghurt.

Warm honey and pecan banana fritters

Serves 4

50 g (1³/4 oz/1 cup) finely crushed cornflakes or rice flakes
40 g (1¹/2 oz/¹/3 cup) finely chopped pecans
1 teaspoon ground cinnamon
55 g (2 oz/¹/4 cup) caster (superfine) sugar
4 bananas, halved
2 tablespoons honey, warmed, to coat
low-fat vanilla icecream or yoghurt, to serve

Preheat the oven to 200°C (400°F/Gas 6). Combine the crushed cornflakes or rice flakes, pecans, cinnamon and sugar in a shallow bowl. Lightly coat the bananas in the honey, then toss them in the cornflake mixture until coated all over. Place the bananas on a baking tray lined with foil or baking paper and lightly spray with a little vegetable oil. Bake for 15–20 minutes, or until hot and golden. Serve with low-fat vanilla icecream or yoghurt.

No-bake fudge cookies

Makes about 40

200 g (7 oz/1¹/3 cups) whole raw unblanched almonds
30 g (1 oz/¹/3 cup) sugar-free whey protein powder
10 fresh dates, stoned
25 g (1 oz/¹/4 cup) desiccated coconut, plus extra
    for coating
30 g (1 oz/¹/4 cup) sunflower seeds
40 g (1¹/2 oz/¹/4 cup) pepitas (pumpkin seeds)
3 heaped tablespoons carob powder
2 tablespoons rice syrup (see Note)
2 heaped tablespoons tahini
1 tablespoon natural vanilla extract
60–125 ml (2–4 fl oz/¹/4–¹/2 cup) apple juice or water

Put the almonds in a food processor and process until
roughly ground. Add the protein powder, dates, coconut,
seeds and carob powder. Process until combined. Add
the rice syrup, tahini and vanilla, then process again. With
the motor still running, add the apple juice or water — just
enough so that the mixture forms a sticky ball. Roll into
walnut-sized portions. Flatten each ball slightly and coat
all or half of the balls in coconut. Store, covered, in the
refrigerator for up to 4 weeks.

Note Brown rice syrup and the similar barley malt syrup
are both available in the health food section in your
supermarket. Their sugars are digested more slowly by
the body, avoiding sugar highs and lows. Their taste is
only mildly sweet. Spread onto toast with a little tahini or
use in place of sugar and honey in dressings.

Oatmeal cookies

Makes 20

1 cup rolled (porridge) oats
45 g (1¹/2 oz/¹/2 cup) desiccated coconut
45 g (1¹/2 oz/¹/2 cup) wheatgerm
75 g (2¹/2 oz/¹/2 cup) wholemeal (whole-wheat) flour
100 g (3¹/2 oz) honey
60 ml (2 fl oz/¹/4 cup) macadamia nut oil
1 teaspoon bicarbonate of soda (baking soda)
3 egg whites

Preheat the oven to 170°C (325°F/Gas 3). Line a baking
tray with baking (parchment) paper.

In a bowl, combine the oats, coconut, wheat germ and
wholemeal flour.

In a small saucepan, heat the honey and macadamia nut
oil until the mixture just comes to the boil. Remove from
the heat and mix in the bicarbonate of soda. As soon as
the mixture froths, pour it into the oat mixture. Fold
together along with the egg whites.

Roll into small balls, put on the prepared baking tray and
flatten a little. Bake for 15 minutes, or until golden. Allow to
cool before eating.

Apple and blueberry muffins

Makes 12

150 g (5^1/$_2$ oz/1 cup) wholemeal (whole-wheat) flour
150 g (5^1/$_2$ oz/1 cup) unbleached plain (all-purpose) flour
3 teaspoons baking powder
1 teaspoon ground cinnamon
100 g (3^1/$_2$ oz) raw (demerara) sugar
60 g (2^1/$_4$ oz) dried apples, chopped
2 eggs or 4 egg whites
335 g (11^3/$_4$ oz/1^1/$_4$ cups) apple sauce
60 ml (2 fl oz/^{1}/$_4$ cup) skim milk
60 ml (2 fl oz/^{1}/$_4$ cup) macadamia nut oil
250 g (9 oz/1^2/$_3$ cups) fresh or frozen blueberries
60 g (2^1/$_4$ oz/^{1}/$_2$ cup) pecans (optional)

Preheat the oven to 180°C (350°F/Gas 4). Grease a 12-hole muffin tin or line the holes with paper cases.

Combine the flour, baking powder, cinnamon, sugar and apple in a bowl. Add the eggs or egg whites, apple sauce, milk and oil. Mix until just combined. Gently fold through the blueberries until just mixed together. Spoon into the prepared tin. Top with the pecans, if using. Bake for 25–30 minutes, or until cooked through and golden.

Note For wheat- and gluten-free muffins substitute the wholemeal flour with gluten-free plain (all-purpose) flour and use a gluten-free baking powder.

Strawberries with mango and banana sorbet

Serves 6

500 g (1 lb 2 oz/3^1/$_3$ cups) strawberries
1 large handful mint
2 mangoes
2 bananas
4 passionfruit

Thread the strawberries onto skewers, alternating with the mint leaves. Cover and refrigerate until ready to serve. Peel the mangoes and bananas and chop into chunks. Place in the freezer for 2 hours.

Put the frozen mango and banana into a food processor and process until smooth. Serve the sorbet with the strawberry skewers, topped with passionfruit pulp.

Lemon and blueberry tart

Serves 12

Base
250 g (9 oz/1²/3 cups) whole unblanched almonds
15 dried figs
30 g (1 oz/¹/4 cup) sunflower seeds
40 g (1¹/2 oz/¹/4cup) pepitas (pumpkin seeds)
juice and zest from 1 lemon

Filling
3 lemons
500 g (1 lb 2 oz/2 cups) low-fat cottage cheese
500 g (1 lb 2 oz/2 cups) low-fat plain yoghurt
175 g (6 oz/¹/2 cup) honey
1¹/2 tablespoons powdered gelatine, dissolved in
    125 ml (4 fl oz/¹/2 cup) boiling water

Topping
2 tablespoons honey
juice and zest from 1 lemon
2 teaspoons cornflour (cornstarch), dissolved in
    2 tablespoons water
310 g (11 oz/2 cups) blueberries

Make the base first. Combine the almonds, figs, seeds and lemon juice and zest in a food processor and process until the mixture comes together. Line a 22 cm (8¹/2 inch) cake tin with baking paper. Roll the base mixture between 2 sheets of baking paper into a circle large enough to cover the base of the cake tin. Carefully lift into the tin.

Next, make the filling. Zest 2 of the lemons and juice all 3 of them. Put the cottage cheese into a food processor and process until smooth. Add the yoghurt, honey, lemon zest and juice, then process again. Add the dissolved gelatine to the filling mixture while the motor is still running and combine well. Pour over the tart base and place into the refrigerator to set for 3–4 hours.

Finally, make the topping. Combine the honey, lemon zest and juice and 185 ml (6 fl oz/³/4 cup) water in a saucepan. Bring to a gentle simmer. Thicken with the cornflour and water mixture. Add the blueberries and stir through. Pour the topping over the filling and allow to set for a further 2 hours in the refrigerator before serving.

Note Vegans can use silken tofu in place of the cottage cheese, soy yoghurt in place of the yoghurt, agar agar in place of the gelatine and maple syrup for the honey.

Chilled red fruit salad

Serves 6

500 g (1 lb 2 oz) strawberries, halved
300 g (10¹/₂ oz) cherries
300 g (10¹/₂ oz) red seedless grapes
200 g (7 oz) raspberries
125 ml (4 fl oz/¹/₂ cup) limoncello liqueur

Combine all the ingredients and allow to sit for 30 minutes in the refrigerator before eating.

Note You can also serve these berries with a scoop of store-bought lemon sorbet.

Peaches in spiced green tea and honey

Serves 6

1 litre (35 fl oz/4 cups) hot green tea, such as
    genmaicha
235 g (8¹/₂ oz/²/₃ cup) honey
3 teaspoons natural vanilla extract
3 star anise
2 cinnamon sticks
6 peaches, blanched and peeled
250 g (9 oz/2 cups) raspberries, to serve
mint, to garnish

Combine the tea, honey, vanilla, star anise and cinnamon in a saucepan and bring to the boil. Cover the pan and reduce the heat to low. Simmer for 15 minutes to allow the spices to infuse into the tea.

Score the skin at the top of the peaches with a small cross. Place the peaches into the spiced green tea and blanch for 30 seconds, or until the skin loosens.

Remove the peaches with a slotted spoon and plunge them into iced water to cool quickly, then peel away the skin. Remove the spices from the green tea liquid, then boil the liquid to reduce it by half.

Place the peaches into a heatproof bowl and pour over the hot tea. Leave to cool to room temperature, turning the peaches occasionally, then refrigerate. Serve the peaches in bowls and spoon over some of the liquid. Sprinkle the raspberries around the peaches and garnish with mint.

Cinnamon-baked apples

Serves 4

80 g (2³⁄₄ oz/¹⁄₂ cup) chopped dates
¹⁄₂ teaspoon ground cinnamon
30 g (1 oz/¹⁄₄ cup) chopped walnuts
zest from 1 orange
4 apples, cored
375 ml (13 fl oz/1¹⁄₂ cups) apple juice
low-fat vanilla yoghurt or custard, to serve

Preheat the oven to 180°C (350°F/Gas 4). Combine the dates, cinnamon, walnuts and orange zest in a bowl. Stuff the apples generously with this mixture and put them into a small baking dish, just large enough to hold the apples. Pour over the apple juice. Bake, uncovered, for 30–40 minutes, or until the apples are soft, but still holding their shape. Serve as they are or with vanilla yoghurt or custard.

Protein power bars

Makes 16–20

100 g (3¹⁄₂ oz/1 cup) rolled (porridge) oats
125 g (4¹⁄₂ oz/1 cup) slivered almonds
25 g (1 oz/¹⁄₄ cup) desiccated coconut
50 g (1³⁄₄ oz/¹⁄₂ cup) sugar-free whey protein
   powder
200 g (7 oz) dried bananas, chopped
200 g (7 oz) figs, sliced
200 g (7 oz) dried fruit medley
125 ml (4 fl oz/¹⁄₂ cup) apple juice

Preheat the oven to 200°C (400°F/Gas 6). Spread the oats, almonds and coconut over 3 separate baking trays lined with foil or baking paper. Place into the oven to lightly toast until golden. Remove and allow to cool.

Put the toasted oats, coconut and almonds into a food processor with the protein powder, dried banana, fig and fruit medley. Process until combined. Add the apple juice and process again until the mixture holds together. Roll or press the mixture between 2 sheets of baking paper until about 1–1.5 cm (¹⁄₂–⁵⁄₈ inch) thick. Leaving the baking paper on, cover with plastic wrap and refrigerate for 1–2 hours.

Remove the plastic wrap and paper and cut into small bite-sized bars. Store, covered, in an airtight container in the refrigerator for up to 4 weeks.

Apple strudel

Serves 8 (Makes 2 strudels)

6 cooking apples, such as granny smith, peeled and
  thinly sliced
100 g (3¹/₂ oz/¹/₃ cup) sugar-free apricot jam,
  warmed
100 g (3¹/₂ oz/1 cup) ground almonds
pinch of ground cinnamon
85 g (3 oz/²/₃ cup) sultanas (golden raisins)
8 sheets filo pastry
1 egg white, beaten
1 tablespoon sugar
low-fat vanilla yoghurt or custard, to serve

Preheat the oven to 180°C (350°F/Gas 4). Put the apple
and jam in a bowl. Mix together until the fruit is lightly
coated in the jam. Add the almonds, cinnamon and
sultanas and fold through.

Lay 4 filo sheets on a baking tray lined with baking paper.
Pile half of the apple mixture into the middle of the pastry,
then roll up into a long log shape, tucking the ends in
underneath. Make a second strudel with the remaining
filo sheets and apple mixture. Brush each strudel with the
combined egg white and sugar. Bake for 25 minutes, or
until the pastry is crisp and golden. Serve warm, on its
own or with a dollop of vanilla yoghurt or custard.

Chai tea poached pears with pink grapefruit salad

Serves 4

350 g (12 oz/1 cup) honey
6 vanilla chai tea bags
4 star anise
4 pears, peeled
4 pink grapefruit, segmented
1 tablespoon chopped pistachio nuts

Put the honey, tea bags, star anise and 1.5 litres (52 fl oz/
6 cups) water into a saucepan. Bring to the boil, then
reduce the heat and simmer over low heat for 15 minutes
to allow the tea to infuse into the water. Remove the tea
bags and add the pears. Simmer for 20–30 minutes,
gently turning the pears occasionally.

Remove the pears from the liquid and set them aside in a
bowl. Reduce the poaching liquid by about two-thirds, or
by enough to give 500 ml (17 fl oz/2 cups) liquid. Pour the
liquid over the pears and allow to cool. Store in the
refrigerator until needed.

Divide the grapefruit segments among serving bowls.
Place a whole poached pear on top. Spoon a little of the
syrup over the pears, then lightly sprinkle with pistachios.

Flourless chocolate cake with dark chocolate sauce

Serves 12

6 eggs, at room temperature, separated
75 g (2¹/2 oz/1¹/2 cups) low-calorie sweetener
2 teaspoons natural vanilla extract
150 g (5¹/2 oz/1¹/2 cups) ground almonds
2 teaspoons baking powder
60 g (2¹/4 oz/¹/2 cup) unsweetened cocoa powder, sifted
60 ml (2 fl oz/¹/4 cup) hazelnut or almond liqueur
200 ml (7 fl oz) light coconut cream
200 g (7 oz) good-quality dark chocolate, chopped
fresh raspberries or strawberries, to garnish (optional)

Preheat the oven to 170°C (325°F/Gas 3). Lightly spray a 23 cm (9 inch) baking tin with vegetable oil and dust with cocoa powder. Beat together the egg whites, sweetener and vanilla until soft peaks form. Beat in the egg yolks, then fold in the ground almonds, baking powder, cocoa and liqueur. Spoon the mixture into the prepared tin. Bake for 25–30 minutes, or until firm to the touch and a skewer inserted into the centre of the cake comes out clean. Allow the cake to cool for 10 minutes in the tin before turning out to cool completely.

To make the dark chocolate sauce, pour the coconut cream into a saucepan and bring to the boil. Turn off the heat and add the chocolate. Stir until the chocolate dissolves into the coconut cream, then allow to cool and thicken. Serve the cake with the chocolate sauce poured over it. Garnish with raspberries or strawberries, if you like.

Yoghurt, honey and vanilla ice cream with grilled banana and passionfruit

Serves 6

1 kg (2 lb 4 oz/4 cups) low-fat plain yoghurt with live cultures
175 g (6 oz/¹/2 cup) honey, warmed
1 tablespoon natural vanilla extract
3 bananas, halved, then quartered
2 tablespoons soft brown sugar or grated palm sugar
125 ml (4 fl oz/¹/2 cup) passionfruit pulp

Mix together the yoghurt, honey and vanilla, then churn in an ice-cream machine according to the manufacturer's instructions, then freeze.

Lay the banana on a baking tray lined with foil and sprinkle lightly with the sugar. Grill (broil) for 1–2 minutes, or until the sugar is golden and bubbling. Serve with a scoop of yoghurt ice cream and some passionfruit spooned over the top.

Note Allow the ice cream to soften for 10 minutes at room temperature before using. Store in a sealed container in the freezer.

Red cherry brownies

Makes 20 pieces

150 g (5$^{1}/_2$ oz/1 cup) wholemeal (whole-wheat) flour
55 g (2 oz/$^{1}/_2$ cup) ground almonds
60 g (2$^{1}/_4$ oz/$^{1}/_2$ cup) unsweetened cocoa powder
1 teaspoon baking powder
pinch of salt
2 teaspoons natural vanilla extract
$^{1}/_4$ teaspoon natural almond extract
125 ml (4 fl oz/$^{1}/_2$ cup) macadamia nut oil or olive oil
185 ml (6 fl oz/$^{3}/_4$ cup) maple syrup
2 egg whites
60 ml (2 fl oz/$^{1}/_4$ cup) low-fat milk or soy milk
80 g (2$^{3}/_4$ oz/$^{1}/_2$ cup) chopped dark chocolate
200 g (7 oz) red cherries, pitted and chopped

Preheat the oven to 170°C (325°F/Gas 3). Line a square 25 cm (10 inch) cake tin with baking paper. Combine the flour, almonds, cocoa, baking powder and salt in a bowl. Add the vanilla and almond extracts, the oil, maple syrup, egg whites, milk, chocolate and cherries. Mix together well, then pour into the prepared cake tin, smoothing the top level.

Bake for 30 minutes, or until firm to the touch and cooked through. Cool to room temperature, then cut into squares. Store the brownies in an airtight container in the refrigerator for up to 5 days.

Chocolate mousse

Serves 12

150 g (5$^{1}/_2$ oz) good-quality dark chocolate
1$^{1}/_2$ tablespoons powdered gelatine
4 egg whites, at room temperature
2 teaspoons natural vanilla extract
25 g (1 oz/$^{1}/_2$ cup) low-calorie sweetener
375 ml (13 fl oz/1$^{1}/_2$ cups) tinned light evaporated
  skim milk, well chilled
2 tablespoons unsweetened cocoa powder
cherries or berries, to serve (optional)

Place the chocolate in a small heatproof bowl set over a saucepan of barely simmering water. Stir occasionally until melted, then remove from the heat. Combine the gelatine and 125 ml (4 fl oz/$^{1}/_2$ cup) water in another bowl, sit it over the simmering water and stir until the gelatine has dissolved.

Beat the egg whites until soft peaks form, then slowly add the vanilla and sweetener, beating well until a thick and glossy meringue forms. Beat the evaporated milk in a separate bowl, until thick and creamy. Add the dissolved gelatine to the meringue mixture and beat well until combined. Add the melted chocolate and beat once again. Add the cocoa and beat a final time.

Spoon the chocolate meringue into the beaten milk and fold through with a large metal spoon. Pour into one large bowl or divide among individual serving bowls. Allow to set in the refrigerator for about 2 hours before serving. Serve alone or with cherries or seasonal berries.

Apple and passionfruit crumbles

Serves 6

Crumble
100 g (3¹/₂ oz/1 cup) rolled (porridge) oats
2 tablespoons flaked coconut
100 g (3¹/₂ oz) cashew nuts, chopped
2 tablespoons honey, warmed

6 apples, peeled and cut into chunks
125 ml (4 fl oz/¹/₂ cup) apple juice
1–2 tablespoons honey, maple syrup or low-calorie
  sweetener
¹/₄ teaspoon ground cinnamon
pulp from 2 passionfruit

Preheat the oven to 180°C (350°F/Gas 4). Spread the oats, coconut and cashew nuts over 3 separate baking trays lined with baking paper. Bake for 10–15 minutes, or until golden brown. Immediately after cooking, put the oats, cashews and coconut into a mixing bowl and stir through the warmed honey. Leave to cool until crisp.

Combine the apples, apple juice, honey, maple syrup or sweetener and cinnamon in a saucepan. Cook over low heat for 20–30 minutes, or until the apples are soft. Add the passionfruit pulp. Mix together lightly with a spoon or fork, but do not overmix. Divide the warm apple mixture among individual serving dishes and sprinkle over the crumble topping.

Note The apple mixture keeps for up to 4 days if stored, covered, in the refrigerator. It's also nice for breakfast with low-fat plain yoghurt. Eat hot or cold.

Banana blueberry cake

Serves 10–12

190 g (6³/₄ oz/1¹/₄ cups) wholemeal (whole-wheat)
  flour
3 teaspoons baking powder
40 g (1¹/₂ oz/¹/₂ cup) wheat germ
50 g (2 oz/¹/₂ cup) vanilla protein powder or skim milk
  powder
1 teaspoon ground cinnamon
2 large bananas, mashed
2 teaspoons natural vanilla extract
4 egg whites, lightly beaten
125 ml (4 fl oz/¹/₂ cup) maple syrup
200 g (7 oz) dried pears, sliced
190 g (6³/₄ oz/1¹/₄ cups) fresh or frozen blueberries

Preheat the oven to 180°C (350°F/Gas 4). Combine the flour, baking powder, wheat germ, protein powder and cinnamon in a bowl. Add the mashed banana, vanilla, egg whites, maple syrup and sliced pears, then fold in the blueberries.

Pour into a medium-sized loaf tin lined with baking paper. Bake for 50 minutes, or until cooked through. Cover the top with foil if necessary to prevent it from browning too much. Remove from the oven and cool for 30 minutes before turning out onto a wire rack to finish cooling. Serve plain or toasted with cottage cheese or ricotta, sliced banana and some honey drizzled over.

Store wrapped in plastic wrap in the refrigerator for up to 5 days.

Blueberry cheesecakes

Makes 8–10

500 g (1 lb 2 oz/2 cups) low-fat cottage cheese or
    silken tofu
90 g (3¼ oz/¼ cup) honey
zest from 1 lemon
2 teaspoons natural vanilla extract
3 egg whites
30 g (1 oz/¼ cup) cornflour (cornstarch)
150 g (5½ oz/1 cup) fresh or frozen blueberries, plus
    extra, to garnish
100 g (3½ oz/1 cup) ground almonds
½ teaspoon ground cinnamon

Preheat the oven to 170°C (325°F/Gas 3). Process the
cottage cheese or tofu in a food processor until smooth.
Add the honey, lemon zest, vanilla and egg whites, then
process again until smooth. Add the cornflour and
process until combined. Fold in the blueberries by hand.

Line individual muffin tins with paper cases (alternatively,
you can use one 20 cm (8 inch) round cake tin). Sprinkle
the combined almonds and cinnamon over the bases.
Spoon in the cheese filling and bake for 25–30 minutes,
or until the tops are firm to the touch. (If made in a cake
tin, it will take 15 minutes longer.) Allow to cool, then chill
before serving, garnished with extra blueberries.

Note Raspberries can be substituted for the blueberries.

Wholemeal carrot cake

Makes 1 loaf

3 eggs
280 g (10 oz/1½ cups) soft light brown sugar
2 teaspoons natural vanilla extract
125 ml (4 fl oz/½ cup) apple sauce
125 ml (4 fl oz/½ cup) macadamia nut oil
700 g (1 lb 9 oz) carrots, grated
500 g (1 lb 2 oz/4 cups) wholemeal (whole-wheat)
    flour
4 teaspoons baking powder
2 teaspoons ground cinnamon
½ teaspoon ground nutmeg
½ teaspoon ground cloves
150 g (5½ oz) pecans or walnuts, chopped
150 g (5½ oz) dried apricots, chopped

Preheat the oven to 180°C (350°F/Gas 4). Grease a large
loaf tin or 25 cm (10 inch) round cake tin and line it with
baking paper. Combine the eggs, sugar, vanilla, apple
sauce and oil in a bowl. Mix through the carrot, then the
flour, baking powder, cinnamon, nutmeg, cloves, nuts
and apricots.

Pour into the prepared tin and bake for 1¼ hours, or until
cooked through. To see if the cake is cooked, insert a
skewer into the centre — it should come out dry. You may
need to cover the top of the cake with foil halfway through
cooking to prevent it from browning too much. Cool
before eating and store in an airtight container in the
refrigerator for up to 5 days.

EXERCISE

The importance of exercise

There are many benefits of doing regular exercise. If you exercise regularly and moderately, it will reward you by slowing the effects of ageing, increasing energy, reducing fatigue, stress and depression, improving circulation, lowering body fat and cholesterol, increasing your immunity and toning muscles.

A combination of cardiovascular, resistance (weight) training and flexibility training will ensure overall fitness and body shaping. The cardio will get you fit and help you lose body fat. Resistance training will increase your metabolic rate by encouraging the growth of lean muscle mass, and will also help shape and sculpt your body. Flexibility training (stretching) will help decrease muscle soreness and increase mobility, reducing the incidence of injury and encouraging the release of toxins in the muscles. *But before you start any exercise program, remember to get yourself checked out by your doctor to make sure your health is in order.*

For those unfamiliar with the gym jargon that is used in this program, a repetition (rep) is the number of times you lift and lower a weight. For example, in a bicep curl you may lift and lower the weight 15 times before completing the exercise; that means you have just completed one set of 15 reps. A superset combines two exercises without rest in between. Giant sets are supersets of more than two exercises carried out without rest in between, like in the group of exercises in the home and gym workouts later in this chapter.

You may sometimes experience slight hypoglycaemia (low blood sugar) during or after exercise, especially in the morning when your blood sugars are at their lowest. Feeling a little weak, dizzy or spaced out is a sign of hypoglycaemia. You may also get palpitations or a light tremor. For most people it's easily controlled by having a quickly absorbed carbohydrate like a small glass of orange juice, a banana, a piece of toast or a cup of tea with honey. If you're diabetic, it's important you eat small regular meals throughout the day and include enough protein and low-GI carbs, which release energy slowly into the bloodstream.

Always vary your workouts. Your body will get used to an exercise routine pretty quickly and sooner or later you'll reach a plateau where nothing much changes. Vary what you do every couple of weeks, and change your intensity levels, as well. If you walk every day, mix it with a little swimming or cycling. If you have a treadmill or stationary bike at home, alternate 3-minute cardio sessions with 20 squats, push-ups and crunches in your lounge room. Do this for 30 minutes and you will have an amazing workout in the comfort of your own home.

You should also introduce a little interval training into your daily cardio routine; increase the intensity of your workout for a couple of minutes, then ease off for a minute. For instance, on your next walk, pick an area where there are lots of hills or stairs to climb, or if you're on a flat surface power-walk for 2 minutes and jog for 1 minute. Or walk briskly for 2 minutes and ease off for 1 minute. Just make it interesting and varied — shock your body!

If you like to walk, invest in a pedometer from a sports store. Wear it every day and aim for at least 10 000 steps a day. It's quite fun and will give you an accurate indication of how active you've been that day.

Also, don't forget incidental exercise in your daily life — this means taking the stairs instead of the lift, using housework or gardening as a workout, walking to work, school or to the shops, walking the dog, or washing your car by hand rather than at the car wash. It doesn't matter what you do; just make movement a part of your day.

Choose active holidays where you can move. Go skiing, cycling or bushwalking, learn how to surf or take up a self-defence or martial arts class. I guarantee that with all the variety, your body will thank you. You'll soon start to look great and feel empowered, strong and in control.

The home workout

Exercising regularly doesn't mean you have to join a gym. You can do a great workout at home — all you need is a soft mat, some light (2–3 kg/4–6 lb) hand weights and a fit ball.

Try to do the home workout 2 or 3 times a week. Begin with a 20-minute cardio session (see page 181 for a list of cardio options that you can choose from, and their calorie-burning capabilities). It's okay if you can only do 5 minutes at first; just gradually increase your time as you become fitter. Don't worry if the total workout takes you longer than 60 minutes; just do the best you can. When doing the home workout, repeat each group twice before moving on to the next group. Always finish the workout with a gentle stretch. This will give your body a chance to cool down and relax. On pages 178–181 there are explanations for each exercise; read through them first to ensure you are familiar with the exercises before you start.

One thing to note with the following workout is that there is no time for rest between sets. If you can't do the required amount in the set time, don't worry — just do as much as you can and aim to increase the number of reps every time you do the workout. Put on your favourite exercise music and do the workout as efficiently as you can without resting. If the exercises leave you a bit sore or tired, take it easier the next day to allow your body to recharge and repair. But most of all, have fun!

It's a good idea to hire a trainer to come to your house for one session to check your form and ensure that you're doing each exercise correctly. If you have an injury, tell your trainer; they can suggest another exercise to work around your injury.

TO BEGIN
20-minute cardio session (walking, skipping, dancing, cycling, jogging, steps)

GROUP 1
Wide squats free standing or with fit ball: 30–50 repetitions
Fit ball leg curl: 20 reps
Wide push-ups: 15–20 reps
Crunches on mat or on fit ball: 20–30 reps

GROUP 2
Dumbbell shoulder press: 30 reps
Dumbbell lateral raises: 30 reps
Fit ball or free lunges: 20 each leg
Side crunches: 20 each side

GROUP 3
Fit ball Russian twist: 20 each side
Dumbbell bicep curls: 30 reps
Tricep chair dips: 20 reps
Supermans: 15 reps

Stretch and cool down.

Exercises for home and gym workouts

SQUATS — To do free-standing squats, have your feet slightly wider than the shoulders. Bend both knees and inhale as you go down, until your thighs are parallel to the floor. Push up again and exhale, focusing on coming up through your heels. Do this in a rhythmical up-and-down motion, with no rest at the top. Keep your shoulders back and your chest and bottom out (as though you're going to sit on a chair). Bring your arms out in front of you as you go down, then back to your sides as you come up. If doing this with a fit ball, have your back against the ball and the ball against the wall for support. Your feet should be out in front. Bend both knees and inhale as you go down, until your thighs are parallel to the floor. Push up again and exhale, focusing on coming up through your heels. Do this in a rhythmical up-and-down motion, with no rest at the top. This is a great leg exercise.

FIT BALL LEG CURL — Lie on your mat on your back with your heels on top of the fit ball. Have your arms resting by your sides, palms down. Lift your bottom off the floor. Roll the ball towards you using your heels, until your knees are above your hips, then roll it back to the starting position. Do this 20 times in a rhythmical back-and-forth motion. This works the back of the legs and the glutes (buttock muscles).

WIDE PUSH-UPS — Lie face down on the floor on your mat, placing your palms on either side of your chest. Put your hands out wide if you want to emphasize working your chest area. Keeping your body straight, press up from the floor, exhaling as you come up. Beginners should be on their knees only — advanced exercisers should be on their toes. Inhaling, lower your body to touch your chin to the floor. Do the push-ups in a rhythmical, smooth, up-and-down motion until you can't do any more. If you find push-ups hard, you can do an easier version of them by standing and pressing up against a wall, or with a fit ball against a wall.

CRUNCHES — Lie on a soft mat on your back with your knees bent and feet flat on the floor. Place your hands on your temples. Keep your head in a neutral relaxed position, remembering not to pull on the head as you come up. Raise the head and shoulders off the floor as far as possible, breathing out as you go. Slowly lower yourself down to the starting position, breathing in and keeping your head off the floor. For a harder crunch, take your hands off your temples and attempt to touch your knees when you come up. Do the crunches in a controlled, rhythmical motion.

DUMBBELL SHOULDER PRESS — Stand with a dumbbell in each hand, held at the side of the head. Stand with your feet shoulder-width apart, the back straight and shoulders back. Lift your arms above your head, exhaling as you go up, and then lower your arms back to the starting position, inhaling as you return to the starting position. This exercise gives strong, shapely shoulders.

DUMBBELL LATERAL RAISES — Stand with your back slightly arched at your lower back and have your shoulders back. Have a dumbbell in each hand, with arms at your sides and elbows slightly bent. Raise your arms out to the sides at shoulder level. Keep your elbows in line with the shoulders and exhale at the same time. Lower the weights back to the starting position, inhaling at the same time. Repeat in a strict rhythmical motion until you have completed the required number of repetitions. This is another great shoulder exercise that gives a lovely shape to the arms.

LUNGES — Place your hands on your hips and take a large step forward with the right leg, lowering your left knee towards the floor (remember not to let the knee go past the toes). Push up again with your right heel and return to the starting position. Repeat with the left leg. Alternate left and right until each leg has completed the exercise 20 times. This exercise is a fantastic workout for the legs and glutes (buttock muscles).

SIDE CRUNCHES — Lie on your back on a mat with your knees bent and feet firmly on the floor. Roll your knees to the side. Support your neck by placing your hands at the side of your temples, keeping your head in a relaxed position looking up at the ceiling. Remember not to pull on the head as you come up. Raise the head and shoulders off the floor as far as possible, exhaling at the same time, then slowly lower yourself down to the starting position, inhaling and keeping your head off the floor. Repeat in a rhythmical motion until you finish the required reps. Then roll over and do the other side. This works the sides of your abdominals.

FIT BALL RUSSIAN TWIST — Lie on your back on the floor or on a mat with your legs and hips bent upwards at a 90-degree angle. Position the fit ball up against the back of your thighs. Place your arms out to the side with palms facing upwards. Slowly roll your legs to the side, until you feel a nice stretch on your lower back, then slowly roll your legs to the other side — keep rolling slowly side to side in a smooth, rhythmical motion until you have completed the required number of repetitions. To increase the resistance, place a weighted medicine ball in between the inner thighs while rolling from side to side. This is an excellent exercise for the abdominals and lower back.

DUMBBELL BICEP CURLS — Stand with your feet slightly apart, or sit on top of a fit ball, shoulders back, and dumbbells held in each hand and palms turned out. Keeping your upper arms close to your body, curl the dumbbells up, breathing out as you lift, then breathing in as you lower the dumbbells back to the starting position. Do not swing the weights, but use a steady, rhythmical motion until you have completed all the reps. Great for toning arms.

TRICEP DIPS — Sit on a sturdy chair or couch with arms placed close to your sides. Place your palms on the chair with hands facing forward. Slowly come out a little way by lifting yourself off and out with your hands, with your feet still bent, then start to lower your bottom to the floor, then raise yourself, pushing up from the palms. Keep your head up and back straight. This tones the back of the arms.

SUPERMANS — This is great for strengthening the lower back. Lie face down on a mat with your arms out in front of you and your legs bent at the knees (your feet and lower legs will be in the air). Slightly lift both your arms and thighs off the floor and hold for 3 seconds, then return to the starting position. (With arms and thighs raised, you will look a bit like you are skydiving.)

LYING DUMBBELL TRICEP EXTENSIONS — Lie down on your back on a flat bench with dumbbells in each hand and arms extended over your head at eye level. Make sure your palms are facing each other. Your feet can either be flat on the floor or raised over the bench, with ankles crossed in front of you. Lower your forearms towards your shoulders, bending the elbows and keeping your upper arms stationary. Press the weight back up to the starting position and repeat until you have completed the required number of reps. This is another great arm toner.

FULL SIT-UPS — This is the classic full sit-up that really works the abdominals (stomach muscles). Start by lying on your back with your knees bent and feet flat on the floor. Arms can be either held lightly to the side of your head for support or crossed in front of your chest. Your head and shoulders should be slightly lifted off the floor in the starting position. Bring your torso towards your knees, hold for a second, then lower your torso back to the floor into the starting position. Make sure to breathe out on the way up and in on the way down.

KNEE RAISES — Lie on your back with your arms at your sides, then tuck your palms down under your bottom. Bend your knees slightly and lift head and shoulders off the floor. This is the starting position. Now draw your knees up to your chest, hold for a second, then lower your legs back to the starting position. Great for your abdominals.

PLANKS — The starting position is like a full push-up, but is supported from your elbows and toes. Your body should be dead straight, without your bottom sticking up in the air. Hold this position for 30–60 seconds. This is a fantastic exercise for the abdominals and core strength.

LYING V CRUNCHES — Lie on your back with legs straight up in the air, feet up towards the ceiling. Your head and shoulders should be off the floor. This is the starting position. Reach up with your hands to touch your toes, then come back down to the starting position. A challenging abdominal exercise.

TICK-TOCKS — These are similar to the Russian twist but without the fit ball. Lie on your back with legs up towards the ceiling and arms out to the side, palms facing down. Take your legs sideways down to about 45 degrees, then back the other way to do the other side. This exercise helps strengthen the abdominals.

ONE-ARM DUMBBELL ROW — Start with your left knee and left hand supporting you on a flat bench, and your right foot on the floor, knee slightly bent and out to the side. Your back should be almost parallel with the floor, your bottom and chest both sticking out. Reach down and pick up a dumbbell with your right hand, pull the dumbbell straight up to your chest, then lower back to the starting position. Concentrate on keeping your wrist straight and pull your elbow straight up. After you've completed the required number of reps, repeat with the other side. This exercise works the back.

LAT PULLDOWN — Start by setting the correct weight and positioning yourself so that your knees fit underneath the knee pads. Grab the bar above you at a point just wider than shoulder-width apart, generally where the bar starts to bend. Pull the bar down to the top of your chest, just at shoulder level, keeping the elbows to the ground and arching the lower back slightly, with your chest sticking out. In a controlled motion, slowly bring the bar back to the starting position and complete the required number of reps. Pulldowns firm and strengthen the back muscles.

BARBELL BICEP CURL — Stand with feet shoulder-width apart, knees slightly bent and shoulders back. Hold the barbell with an underhand grip and arms extended out slightly. Hands should be placed on the barbell about shoulder-width apart. This is your starting position. Slowly curl the bar up towards your shoulders, keeping your elbows close to your sides. Lower back to the starting position and repeat until you've completed the required number of reps. Do not swing the weights, but use a smooth, rhythmical motion. These help to tone and shape the arms.

INCLINE DUMBBELL CHEST PRESS — Lie down on your back on an incline bench, holding a dumbbell in each hand. Hold the dumbbells to the side near the shoulders with palms facing forward and elbows down. Press the weights straight up, without locking the elbows, then return to the starting position. Don't allow the weights to swing towards your face, and keep your head on the bench. Complete the required number of reps in a smooth, controlled motion. Remember to breathe out when pushing the weights up. These tone and shape the chest and arms.

INCLINE DUMBBELL FLYS — Lie down on an incline bench, holding a dumbbell in each hand. Raise your arms straight out above your chest, palms facing each other and elbows slightly bent. Lower the dumbbells in an arc and away from the body until your hands are in line with the bench or the sides of your body. Slowly raise the weights back up using the same curve motion until they are above your chest again. When doing this exercise, imagine you're giving someone a big hug. Complete the required number of reps in a controlled motion. Inhale as you move the weights down and exhale as you bring the weights back in. This exercise tones and shapes the chest.

After the workout, give yourself 10–15 minutes to cool down. Gently stretch out all your muscle groups, holding each stretch for about 30 seconds. See page 187 for some simple stretch exercises. Breathe in deeply and breathe out to relax yourself and allow your body to calm down. Drink plenty of water afterwards and have a healthy breakfast.

Cardio suggestions

The following gives a rough guide to the calories that will be used in 30 minutes of activity. The amount of calories burnt will increase as you up the intensity.

Aerobics 200	Ice skating 200	Table tennis 130
Badminton 195	Jogging 250	Tae kwon do 170
Ballet 170	Karate 220	Tai chi 130
Basketball 220	Kickboxing 350	Tennis 275
Boxing 300	Mowing the lawn 150	Volleyball 220
Brazilian jujitsu 300	Muay Thai kickboxing . . . 350	Walking (the dog or
Canoeing 200	Netball 220	with a pram) 150
Cycling or taking a	Painting the house 170	Walking briskly 200
spin class 220	Rollerblading 230	Washing the car 150
Dancing 200	Rugby 300	Washing windows 150
Football 270	Sex 150	Water aerobics 140
Gardening 150	Skiing (snow) 350	Water polo 350
Golf 130	Skipping 340	Water skiing 220
Hiking 200	Soccer 340	Whitewater rafting 180
Horse riding 250	Stair climbing 300	Working out in the gym . . 190
House cleaning 120	Surfing 220	Yoga and pilates 180
Ice hockey 230	Swimming 300	

The home workout timetable

Below is a rough outline of what your average week should look like. Move the days around to fit in with your lifestyle if you need to. Rest and play days are there for you to recharge and have fun. Relax, go to the movies, have a massage, go for a walk in the park or on the beach — allow your body to rest and repair. If you're feeling energetic, by all means do more cardio.

MONDAY	Home workout (including 20 minutes cardio)
TUESDAY	60 minutes cardio workout — your choice
WEDNESDAY	Home workout (including 20 minutes cardio)
THURSDAY	60 minutes cardio workout — your choice
FRIDAY	Home workout (including 20 minutes cardio)
SATURDAY	Rest or play — just have fun
SUNDAY	Rest or play — just have fun

On the days you don't do your home training, you should try to do other fat-burning exercises that complement your home workout. By fat-burning I mean any exercise that requires you to move those large muscle groups, such as walking, jogging, cycling, roller-blading, skipping, boxing and rowing. If you can't leave the house, get yourself a treadmill or stationary bike — they're fantastic fat burners. If you're up to the challenge and want something different, set up a boxing bag in the garage and get yourself a pair of good boxing gloves. Get some lessons from a personal trainer or at the local gym, so that you know some basic boxing and kickboxing techniques and combinations. Write them down so you won't forget. Do a little skipping to warm up, then do your thing on the bag for 2 minutes. Have 30 seconds rest, and then do it again. Remember to keep your combinations simple so you won't get confused. Finish off with a few sets of crunches and a good stretch.

The gym workout

Resistance or weight training is an important factor in increasing metabolic rate since muscle mass is increased through resistance training. The more muscle tissue you have in your body the faster your metabolic rate. So a combination of aerobic exercise (cardio), which helps burn body fat and maintain cardiovascular fitness, combined with regular resistance training and good eating habits is the best combination to generate fat loss.

When working with weights, I find light weights and high repetitions (20–50 reps) work best for women and those who want extreme-fat burning and toning. Try not to rest much in between sets to keep the heart rate elevated. Make sure to keep hydrated with regular sips of water.

Men can choose weights according to their strength capabilities. For weight loss and overall body conditioning, aim for 15–20 repetitions with little rest in between each exercise. For muscle building, aim for 8–12 repetitions with 60 seconds rest in between each superset or giant set of exercises. For those who want to work extra hard, you can choose to do crunches in between the short rest periods to keep your heart rate elevated.

Remember to keep your ego in check when using weights — don't be a hero, or you're likely to give yourself an injury. Make sure to have good control when working out with weights, and maintain a constant, even speed during your repetitions.

Before you try any exercise program, make sure to consult your doctor for a full check-up and have a trainer check your form to ensure that you're doing each exercise correctly. Also, if you have an injury, tell your instructor and have them suggest another exercise to work around your injury.

At least 20 minutes of cardio is also needed before a weights session to warm up and for maximum fat-burning.

Women's workout timetable

MONDAY	20 minutes cardio + full body weights workout
TUESDAY	60 minutes cardio
WEDNESDAY	60 minutes cardio
THURSDAY	20 minutes cardio + full body weights workout
FRIDAY	60 minutes cardio
SATURDAY	Rest and play
SUNDAY	Rest and play

Women's workout

Complete each group of exercises without rest, then repeat. Move to group 2, complete without rest and repeat. Move onto group 3, complete without rest and repeat. Once your body gets used to the exercises and your fitness increases, you will be able to complete each group 3 times.

TO BEGIN: 20-minute cardio session

GROUP 1

Free-standing squats: 50 reps
Lunges: 20 each leg
Dumbbell shoulder press: 30 reps
Dumbbell lateral raises: 30 reps

GROUP 2

Incline dumbbell chest press: 30 reps
Push-ups: 20 reps
One-arm dumbbell rows: 30 reps
Crunches: 30 reps

GROUP 3

Dumbbell bicep curls: 30 reps
Tricep dips: 15 reps
Fit ball Russian twist: 20 reps
Planks — hold for 30–60 seconds

Stretch and cool down.

Men's workout

The men's workout focuses on training the full body once during the course of the week. You must also include 20 minutes of cardio before you start the workout. This will not only help burn body fat, but it will also allow your body to warm up before the weights workout. Complete each group of exercises then repeat 2 more times. Move to group 2 and complete the group of exercises, then repeat twice more. After a month you can increase the exercises from 3 sets to 4 sets. Remember 15–20 reps for weight loss, or do 8–12 for muscle building.

Men's workout timetable

MONDAY	20 minutes cardio + legs, shoulders, abs
TUESDAY	60 minutes cardio
WEDNESDAY	20 minute cardio + chest, biceps, abs
THURSDAY	60 minutes cardio
FRIDAY	20 minute cardio + back, triceps, abs
SATURDAY	Rest and play
SUNDAY	Rest and play

Monday's program: Legs, shoulders, abs

TO BEGIN: 20-minute cardio session

GROUP 1

Squats: 15–20 reps
Lunges: 15–20 each leg
Crunches: 30 reps (use crunches as your rest; after that, move straight into another set of squats and lunges)

GROUP 2

Dumbbell shoulder press: 15–20 reps
Dumbbell lateral raises: 15–20 reps
Lying V crunches: 30 reps (use the crunches as your rest; after that, move straight into another set of shoulder press and raises)

Stretch and cool down.

Wednesday's program: Chest, biceps, abs

Complete each group of exercises, then repeat 2 more times. Move to group 2 and complete the group of exercises then repeat 2 more times. After a month you can increase the exercises from 3 sets to 4 sets.

TO BEGIN
20-minute cardio session

GROUP 1
Incline dumbbell chest press: 15–20 reps
Incline dumbbell flys: 15–20 reps
Push-ups: 15–20 reps
Tick-tocks: 20

GROUP 2
Barbell bicep curls: 15–20 reps
Dumbbell bicep curls: 12–15 reps
Planks: hold for 30–60 seconds

Stretch and cool down.

Friday's program: Back, triceps, abs

Complete each group of exercises, then repeat twice more. Move to group 2 and complete the group of exercises then repeat twice more. After a month you can increase the exercises from 3 sets to 4 sets.

TO BEGIN
20-minute cardio session

GROUP 1
Lat pulldown: 15–20 reps
One-arm dumbbell row: 12–15 reps
Supermans: 15 reps

GROUP 2
Lying dumbbell tricep extension: 15–20 reps
Tricep dips: 15–20 reps
Sit-ups: 20–30 reps

Stretch and cool down.

Stretching for flexibility

Flexibility training (stretching) should be part of your daily fitness routine. It helps decrease muscle soreness and increases your mobility, reducing the rate of injury. Stretching also encourages the release of toxins in the muscles as well as increasing the blood supply and nutrients to the area. Basically, being flexible will help you perform and enjoy life much more. Here are a few simple stretches to do and tips for safety when performing your stretch.

- Only stretch when muscles are warmed up.
- Do not over-stretch. You should be able to feel the stretch but it should not be painful.
- Breathe slowly, deeply and evenly during the stretch.
- Hold the stretch in a comfortable position for about 60 seconds.
- Avoid bouncy, jerky movements.
- Pregnant women should only undertake flexibility training under supervision.

CALF STRETCH — Stand facing in front of a wall with your palms touching the wall. Place your left foot behind, and flatten your heel to the ground, keeping your leg straight. Hold the stretch for 60 seconds and repeat with the other leg. Repeat the stretch again.

QUADRICEP (FRONT THIGH) STRETCH — Stand in an upright position. Lift your right leg and grab your right ankle with your right hand and slowly pull it towards your bottom. Bring your knees together and contract your tummy muscles. Keep your back straight and hold onto a wall if necessary for balance. Hold for 60 seconds and repeat with the other leg. Repeat the whole stretch again. You should feel the stretch in the front of your thigh.

LYING HAMSTRING STRETCH (BACK OF THE THIGH) STRETCH — Lie down on your back and straighten your right leg. Place a towel over your right foot and slowly pull the leg towards you, until you feel the stretch in your hamstrings. Hold for 60 seconds and repeat with the left leg.

GLUTE (BUTTOCK MUSCLE) STRETCH — Lie down on your back and cross your left ankle over your right knee. Bend your right knee and grasp your right shin with your hands. Slowly pull your knee towards you, then hold for 60 seconds. Repeat with the other leg.

BACK AND SHOULDER STRETCH — While standing, feet shoulder-width apart, cross both arms across your body to grip the elbows of your opposite arms. Rotate gently to the left until you feel the stretch at the back of your right shoulder joint and upper back. Hold for 60 seconds and rotate to the other side. Repeat the whole stretch again.

CHEST AND ARM STRETCH — While standing, feet shoulder-width apart, place your arms by your sides. Bring the arms up to shoulder height. Slowly bring both arms to the back of the body as far as possible, until you feel a stretch on your chest. Try to bring the back of your hands together while keeping your arms straight. Hold the stretch for about 60 seconds and repeat

Conclusion

After reading this book, you will be equipped with the right tools to get you started and on the way to a healthy, fit, lean body. You will be moving forward with a positive attitude and ready to embrace life. It's important to realize that none of us is perfect and there will definitely be ups and downs. But the key word to remember is persistence. If you persist in anything long enough and want it badly enough you WILL achieve your goals in anything you want to do. Congratulations on taking the first step to a healthy lifestyle. You deserve it!

I would love for all of you to share your success stories and progress with me, so please feel free to contact me via my web address: www.teresacutter.com.

Live your life and make your dreams come true.

Love,

Teresa Cutter
'the healthy chef'

Index

Published by Murdoch Books Pty Limited

Murdoch Books Australia
Pier 8/9, 23 Hickson Road, Millers Point NSW 2000
Phone: +61 (0)2 8220 2000 Fax: +61 (0)2 8220 2558

Murdoch Books UK Limited
Erico House, 6th Floor North, 93–99 Upper Richmond Road
Putney, London SW15 2TG
Phone: + 44 (0) 20 8785 5995 Fax: + 44 (0) 20 8785 5985

Chief Executive: Juliet Rogers
Publisher: Kay Scarlett

Concept: Vivien Valk and Lauren Camilleri
Project manager: Janine Flew
Editor: Margaret Malone
Designer: Lauren Camilleri
Photographer: Paul Cutter
Production: Monika Paratore

National Library of Australia Cataloguing-in-Publication Data.
Cutter, Teresa, 1968- . 80/20 diet : 12 weeks to a better body. Includes index.
ISBN 1 74045 647 5. 1. Diet therapy. 2. Cookery. I. Cutter, Paul. II. Title. 615.854

ISBN 1-74045-647-5

Printed by Toppan Printing Hong Kong Co. Ltd. PRINTED IN CHINA. First printed in 2005.

IMPORTANT: Those who might be at risk from the effects of salmonella poisoning (the elderly, pregnant women,
young children and those suffering from immune deficiency diseases) should consult their doctor
with any concerns about eating raw eggs.

CONVERSION GUIDE: You may find that cooking times vary depending on the oven you are using. For fan-forced ovens,
as a general rule, set the oven temperature to 20° C (36° F) lower than indicated in the recipe. We have used 20 ml
(4 teaspoon) tablespoon measures. If you are using a 15 ml (3 teaspoon) tablespoon for most recipes, the difference
will not be noticeable. However, for recipes using baking powder, gelatine, bicarbonate of soda (baking soda) or small
amounts of flour and cornflour (cornstarch), add an extra teaspoon for each tablespoon specified.